SHIPWRECKS AT THE GOLDEN GATE

To Bernard & Elizabeth

Stephen A Haller

12/12/12

SHIPWRECKS AT THE GOLDEN GATE

A History of Vessel Losses from Duxbury Reef
to Mussel Rock

James P. Delgado and Stephen A. Haller

First edition
Copyright © 1989 James P. Delgado and Stephen A. Haller

Published by Lexikos

Edited by Laurie Cohn

Design and Production by Mark Adamsbaum

Cover Illustration by Richard Sigberman

Set in 11 point Palatino. Reproduced from pages generated on
the Macintosh II computer and printed on the Apple
LaserWriter QMS-PS 810.

ISBN 0-938530-49-6 Paper

ISBN 0-938530-50-X Cloth

Printed in the United States of America

Dedication

This is for Mary and Janet.

The four-masted bark Gifford aground at Mussel Rock. With tattered sails still set, Gifford lies broadside to the beach.

Waves batter the port quarter of the freighter Ohioan, *ashore at Point Lobos nest to the Sutro Baths.*

Acknowledgements

Many friends, colleagues, and acquaintances formed the inspiration and helped in the research and writing of this book. Foremost in our gratitude is Dave Buller, sport diver, historian, and the first person to share with us his tales of San Francisco's wrecks. Capt. Bob Daly, retired pilot, helped greatly with the tales of many wrecks, including his adventures aboard *Frank H. Buck*, lost in 1937. Capt. Raymond Aker, the late Harry Dring, and Harlan Soeten told countless stories, corrected errors, and proved able tutors in all aspects of ships, shipping, and the sea. Karl Kortum, former director of the San Francisco Maritime Museum, provided insights on many vessels, particularly the two-masted schooners, steam schooners, and square-riggers that are his passion. John B. Goodman III of Beverly Hills, biographer of hundreds of gold rush vessels, sent information on *Ann Parry* and other 1849 arrivals in California.

Colleagues at the Golden Gate National Recreation and the newly formed San Francisco Maritime National Historical Park (once part of GGNRA) helped with hours of research, both in the archives and library and on park beaches and beneath the cold waters of the Pacific. Martin Mayer, the park archaeologist, was an indefatigable companion while working on *SS Tennessee*, *King Philip*, *Reporter*, the *Lawrence* survey, and countless dives off Alcatraz. Doug Nadeau, chief of resource management and planning for GGNRA, is the park's primary supporter of shipwreck research; his support and guidance helped us leap over bureaucratic hurdles. Brian O'Neill, Superintendent of GGNRA, and his predecessors Bill Whalen and Jack Davis, supported shipwreck research at GGNRA, as did Maritime Unit Manager Glennie Wall, who recognized the importance of shipwrecks to the maritime story of San Francisco and supported research and the first temporary exhibit at the maritime museum, "Shipwrecks of the Golden Gate." Jean Swearingen, now the National Park Service's regional curator for Alaska, designed and supervised that exhibit's creation and became a fast friend and shipwreck story-sharer. Steve Canright, Richard Everett, John Maounis, Herb Beckwith, Kramer Adams, Dave Hull, Sara Halaj, Mike Richards, Dorothea Lyman, and many others at the maritime museum shared finds in the archives, clipping files and collections, or helped identify shipwrecks on the beach.

Volunteers Robert L. Bennett, Gregory Brown, Dave and Steve Buller, Rebecca LaFontaine, and others worked in the field on the wrecks. The discovery and documentation of shipwrecks was also assisted and supported by two members of the NPS Submerged Cultural Resource Unit, Dan Lenihan and Larry Murphy, who are good friends and teachers of shipwreck archaeology. Other historians working on shipwrecks or other aspects of maritime history graciously provided research and advice. We particularly want to thank Robert J. Schwendinger, Max L. O'Starr, Louise Teather, Nick Dean, and Capt.

Bob Daly. We especially appreciate the help of the late Jack Mason of the *Point Reyes Historian*.

The staffs of many institutions provided help: The California Historical Society; the Society of California Pioneers; San Francisco History Room and Archives at the San Francisco Public Library; Federal Archives and Records Center, San Bruno; the National Archives; Mystic Seaport Museum; The Mariners' Museum; South Street Seaport; Marin County Historical Society; California State Library; and the Bancroft Library. We particularly want to thank John Vandereedt and Bill Sherman at the National Archives; Debbie Ginsberg, Roger Jobson, and Grace Baker of the Society of California Pioneers, Judy Sheldon, Waverly Lowell and Gerald Wright of the California Historical Society; and Gladys Hansen of the San Francisco History Room.

Roberto Albanese of Beard's Books suggested Mike Witter and Lexikos as a publisher. Roberto's good advice is gratefully acknowledged, as is the support of Mike Witter. Joy Waldron Murphy carefully edited the text. We are very grateful for her firm but friendly editorial hand. Last but not least we want to thank our wives, Mary and Janet, for their support and encouragement. The patience and understanding of our families made this book possible.

Table of Contents

Frank Buck

Coast Guardsmen from the Bolinas Bay Lifeboat Station assist the failed attempt to salvage the sinking and partially capsized steam schooner Yosemite off the northern Marin coast on February 7, 1926.

Introduction

Maritime Development On The Pacific Coast, 1542-1945

The Spanish conquest and settlement of Mexico in the early years of the sixteenth century opened the Pacific Ocean to Spain's mariners. By mid-century, voyages of exploration had probed the California coast and turned west across the Pacific to the Orient. In 1542 Juan Rodriguez Cabrillo, a veteran of the Mexican conquest, "discovered" California's shores. Others followed Cabrillo, opening a trade route between the Philippines and Mexico in 1565, allowing Spain to finally realize Columbus' dream of a new trade route with the Indies. The California shore was a frequent sight for the crews of the "Manila galleons" that sailed between Manila and Acapulco; a prominent landmark was the *Punta de los Tres Reyes* (Point Reyes). One of the Manila captains, Sebastian Rodriguez Cermeno, arrived at Point Reyes in 1595 to chart the coast for a suitable harbor. His ship, *San Agustin*, dragged ashore in a gale while at anchor in Drakes Bay. Cermeno and his crew abandoned the wreck and took to the sea in an open boat, sailing past the Farallon Islands to safety in Mexico. Sebastian Vizcaino sailed up the California coast in 1602, landing at Monterey Bay and stopping briefly at Drakes Bay to see what could be salvaged from *San Agustin*. His visit was the last in the region for more than a century.

The entrance to San Francisco Bay eluded explorers sailing along California's shores. The narrow harbor entrance at the Golden Gate was one obstacle. The foothills on the bay's eastern side also concealed the harbor. Furthermore, early mariners sailed well out to sea past the Farallones to avoid shipwreck and were too far afield to spot the harbor entrance. Following the discovery of the bay in 1769 and the 1775 voyage of *San Carlos*, Spanish authorities decided that the bay's settlement and defense were essential to regional control. In 1776, they constructed a presidio and mission at the future site of San Francisco, marking the northernmost limit of Spanish imperial expansion in North America. Soon supply ships began making voyages from Mexico to the Golden Gate.

The years of Spanish and Mexican control in California (1769-1846) saw increasing numbers of American vessels come to engage in the fur trade or whaling, or to trade China goods for California's abundant hides and tallow from the vast herds of cattle kept at various private ranchos. Vessels from other nations, many of them South American traders, also called at California ports for hides and tallow. The booming hide trade gave rise to a new port in 1835, when William A. Richardson, formerly a British mariner turned Mexican rancher, founded the small settlement of Yerba Buena on the San Francisco peninsula. Richardson's Yerba Buena was a small but busy hide-trading town, and grew to a village of four hundred by 1846. That year the United States and Mexico declared war. Yerba Buena was an early prize of the Mexican War, and in 1847 was renamed "San Francisco" by its military-appointed *alcalde* (mayor).

Maritime trade in the region dwindled during the war years of 1846-1848, but revived following California's discovery of gold in 1848. The primacy of San Francisco as the principal port on the West Coast was confirmed, as thousands of vessels made their way to San Francisco during the gold rush. The great inland harbor proved to be a relatively safe haven for the vessels. The great rivers piercing California's interior drained into the bay, providing easy waterborne access to the Sierra foothills—and the gold "diggin's." In response to gold rush traffic, San Francisco became a major metropolis. As the principal port, it provided anchorage for hundreds of vessels and a way station for goods bound for the gold fields. The Pacific Coast, otherwise isolated from the rest of the world until the completion of the transcontinental railroad in 1869, depended on ships as the connecting link with civilization, ships that brought raw and manufactured goods, immigrants, and capital.

Natural features in California helped develop the maritime commerce in the San Francisco Bay Area. Before good roads connected the far-flung reaches of the Bay Area to other parts of the nation, and before railroads branched up and down the coast and linked the settlements there, sailing was the most efficient form of transportation between communities isolated from each other by mountains and rivers. San Francisco in particular depended on shipborne goods in its periods of rapid growth. Lumber, bricks, food, machinery, and labor all came from somewhere else because San Francisco and the rest of California yielded scant agriculture and industry. As industry and agriculture began in California, the important role of maritime trade and commerce changed. The Pacific Coast was no longer just a consumer, but a productive partner. Reciprocal trade burgeoned with the establishment of lumber mills, farms, factories, and ranches.

Small craft had a part to play. For local cargos, flat-bottomed scow schooners carried goods in bulk across the far-flung reaches of the bay's shallows. These small, two-masted craft were the bay's workhorses, carrying hay, produce, and lumber to market from mudflat harbors and estuaries. The bay and the waters of the Pacific were harvested for food. Large fleets of fishing vessels based at San Francisco, Monterey, and other ports soon flocked to the coast. From the junks of Chinese fishermen to the sailing feluccas of Mediterranean immigrants, and finally to the gasoline-powered Monterey boats and the diesel-engined trawlers of modern times, fishing craft through the decades were important participants in the maritime commerce of the Pacific coast.

The decline of Atlantic whaling grounds and the growth of San Francisco opened the Pacific Coast to America's whaling fleet. The completion of coast-to-coast rail linkage allowed whale oil and baleen unloaded in San Francisco to be transported to Eastern markets while the vessels stayed west for numerous seasons in succession. By the 1870s San Francisco was the undisputed whaling capital of the United States.

Dozens of whalers sailed and steamed from the city each year for the North Pacific and Arctic whaling grounds. In 1871 much of the Pacific whaling fleet was caught and crushed in the Arctic ice, but more efficient steam whalers, many built at San Francisco, carried on the work. But the near extinction of the species, the ascendency of petroleum oil, and the replacement of whalebone corset stays with metal springs combined to doom the industry. The last outpost of American whaling, a shoreside facility in Richmond on San Francisco Bay, closed in the 1970s.

As gold rush emigrants settled down to more stable lives, many chose to farm the fertile and sunny areas of the great Central Valley or the California Delta. By the 1870s California grain was an important commodity in worldwide trade. Markets on the Eastern Seaboard demanded grain, and the railroads were not able to ship such bulky cargo at competitive rates with cargo vessels. The growing populations of Europe, whose lands were periodically ravaged by warfare, also clamored for wheat cargos. Around Cape Horn from New York, Liverpool, and elsewhere, stately square-riggers arrived in San Francisco every fall, participants in a second "gold rush" for golden wheat. The square-riggers brought coal or manufactured goods of every description to trade for 100-pound sacks of wheat. Many of the granite cobblestones that once lined San Francisco's streets came as ballast in these ships.

The rich groves of redwood and Douglas fir along the coast sparked a busy lumber trade, supplying San Francisco and other growing urban areas on the West Coast. The trade eventually expanded to meet the lumber needs of the world. As early as the 1860s,

more than three hundred mills operated in the redwood forests of northern California. A steadily increasing demand for rot-resistant redwood, and later for northwest fir and pine, was assured by the need for railroad ties. The demand for building material was guaranteed particularly in the wake of the San Francisco earthquake and fire of 1906 and the great construction boom in Southern California.

Throughout the active years of the lumber trade, ships were used for transport. The expense of constructing wagon roads and railroads to the forests was avoided by the cheaper and more expedient means — ships. At first, conditions were difficult. Ships built for other purposes were used, but by the 1870s West Coast shipyards had settled on the general characteristics needed for the specialized conditions of the coastal lumber trade. Large two- and three-masted schooners were built and rigged "bald-headed" without topsails for ease of handling and in order to beat north against prevailing winds. The simple rig of these schooners also allowed for large deckloads of lumber and for ease of loading and unloading. Their shallow draft and sturdy build served well when crossing the sandbars that protect many West Coast ports, or when lying anchored in one of the "dog holes," small anchorages for loading lumber on the northern California coast.

Owners began adding steam engines to lumber schooners around 1880. Shrewd speculator and shipping entrepreneur Robert Dollar built the first intentional steam schooner, *Newsboy*, in 1888. Although sailing schooners lingered on, the sturdy steam schooner proved to be the mainstay of West Coast shipping, many making the transition from lumber to general cargo carriers late in life. As old wooden ships were retired, steel-hulled freighters were pressed into service by the same companies that had originally carried lumber. These vessels carried dry cargoes like sugar, salt, and concrete more safely than a leaky wooden hull. From the 1920s through the 1940s, freighters carried on the coastal trade alongside a few hardy wooden veterans of days gone by. Freighters also ultimately replaced the large wood, iron, and steel sailing ships that had carried goods from Europe, South America, and the Orient in exchange for California products.

Seaborne transportation of people to California peaked between 1848 and 1869 as the initial boom of gold rush migration continued. More than 500,000 persons arrived at or departed San Francisco by Pacific Mail steamers and their competitors. Coastal steamers carried passengers from San Francisco to intermediate ports, such as San Diego, Santa Barbara, Monterey, Eureka, Portland, and Seattle. Smaller, shallow-draft river steamers linked San Francisco with Sacramento and the other cities in California's heartland. The steam schooners developed in the 1880s for the lumber trade also linked passengers with the numerous small lumber mill towns and ports. After 1867 the Pacific Mail Steamship Company commenced regular trans-Pacific service, opening San Francisco to greater trade and immigration from Asia. As the transcontinental railroad and coastal railroads connected California and the Pacific Coast with the rest of the United States, the emphasis on passenger shipping shifted to the trans-Pacific routes and luxury recreational cruises, which continue to this day.

The Great Depression had a devastating impact on the Pacific steamship lines. Coupled with the effects of the Depression were the crippling waterfront strikes across the nation in the 1930s, and especially the General Strike of 1934 that shut down the San Francisco waterfront and much of the rest of the city. The Dollar Line went bankrupt, and with the intervention of the newly established United States Maritime Commission, was succeeded by American President Lines. This line, as well as Matson, Pacific Far East, and others, continued trans-Pacific cargo and passenger trade through the Second World War and into the decades after the war.

Just as politics and economics greatly changed the nature of Pacific coast shipping, so did internal-combustion technology. The rich oil fields of California spawned many oil companies. The development of processing facilities on San Francisco Bay insured the harbor's continued use even though other oil-rich harbors in Southern California, particularly San Pedro, surpassed San Francisco. Beginning in the 1920s, oil, gasoline, and kerosene tankers increasingly steamed to and from San Francisco, San Pedro, and Ventura. As the need for larger cargoes increased, larger and more complex tankers were built, culminating in the modern supertankers that call at the San Francisco Bay ports of Richmond and Benicia.

Since the Second World War, the American merchant marine has declined, and ships that call at San Francisco are usually from distant ports. No ships have been built alongside San Francisco Bay since the early 1970s, and the vessel repair business is a faint ghost of its former self. Air travel, and the expansion of interstate highways, confirmed San Francisco's decline as a seaport. A concurrent revolution in cargo handling doomed older bulk freighters as containerization contributed to the success of Oakland.

Now tankers, container ships, and bulk grain carriers are likely to bypass San Francisco in favor of ports in the East Bay or Stockton — if not to the extensive harbor facilities of Long Beach and Los Angeles. Yachts, fishing boats, and an occasional naval vessel are the usual denizens of San Francisco Bay's waters — much of the other vessel traffic is "just passing through." Beneath the waters of the Golden Gate, however, lie the physical traces of a significant maritime past.

Unidentified salvors on the deck of the bark Gifford. *A steam pump behind them attests to the struggle to save the stranded vessel.*

The United States Lifesaving Service station on Ocean Beach responded to dozens of wrecks and strandings on San Francisco's western shore.

Shipwrecks At The Golden Gate

North of Santa Cruz the California coast runs along a rocky shoreline uninterrupted until the great indentation running from Point San Pedro to Point Reyes. First described by a Spanish navigator, "The Gulf of the Farallones," is bounded to the west by the Farallon Islands and to the east by the Golden Gate. Into these waters have sailed thousands of ships, most bound for the reknowned port of San Francisco. Geographer and historian George Davidson, the first to chart the Gulf of the Farallones, noted that through these waters sailed the "commerce of the world."

San Francisco Bay was discovered in 1769 when a lost party of Spanish explorers spotted it from the hills of San Mateo County. Expeditions that followed in 1770, 1772, and 1775 began to map the bay, and in doing so discovered the harbor entrance. Once the Golden Gate was located, Spanish authorities in Mexico dispatched a ship to chart and name the bay's features. Commanded by Juan Manuel de Ayala, the arrival of the packet *San Carlos* marked the first entrance of a vessel into San Francisco Bay on August 6, 1775.

Since that summer day in 1775, thousands of ships have sailed to the Golden Gate. Hundreds of vessels have come to grief on its rocky shores, wide sandy beaches, or fast currents. Vessels completely wrecked in the Gulf of the Farallones tell stories of life and death. This is the story of ninety-five vessels lost near the Golden Gate. Although twice that number stranded, collided, capsized, or even sank, those vessels were rescued, so their story is not told here. Instead we are looking at shipwrecks underwater or buried beneath the sand.

Ships have been lost off the Golden Gate for many reasons. Some masters mistook the weather. Some were bold when caution should have prevailed. There were those who hesitated when quick action was needed. A few captains may have deliberately wrecked their ships. In late 1862 an old salt's "reflections on the case of shipwrecks" was published in the *California Nautical Magazine*, claiming that a great many wrecks were caused solely by human error compounded by unforgiving tides, currents, and winds. He listed the errors: "neglect of the lead, bad lookout, being short-handed, navigating by dead reckoning, neglect of tides, or ignorance of their direction, mistaking the land, collision, employment of pilots who are not seamen. . . . and shaving headlands too close in rounding them with an on-shore wind." However, often the sailing conditions at the Golden Gate was the sole cause of disaster. Many ships wrecked on the treacherous bar. Strong, shifting currents and tides took others at the narrow entrance to the harbor.

Other ships wrecked in the fog that blankets the coast. San Francisco's Mediterreanean climate, characterized by only two seasons, causes fog. A warm, dry season in California lasts from April to October, when prevailing northwest winds condense near the coast as they blow across cold offshore waters. A thick fog belt forms over the water and presses in to blanket the bay for days at a time. A season of changeable weather lasts from November to April. Then, the temperature is colder although still moderate, and rainstorms with southerly winds occur, followed by periods of mild and sunny weather.

The Japan Current runs southward along the coast, carrying cold waters from Alaska, contrasting with warmer waters farther offshore, and contributing to the summer fog. Prevailing northwesterly winds blow from the ocean toward the shore and greatly increase the hazard of navigation along the coast. The prevailing winds caused most shipwrecks along San Francisco's western shore on Ocean Beach and the Northern Marin County coastline.

The coast is equally exposed when winter storms blow in southerly winds. Except for San Francisco Bay, there are no safe deepwater anchorages protected from that direction. Shallow and restricted anchoring places for small craft exist at Bodega Bay, Tomales Bay, Drakes Bay, and Bolinas Bay, but larger vessels seeking haven there have often succumbed.

Compounding the dangers of navigating this lee shore with its scarcity of sheltered harbors is the rocky shoreline. A vessel in distress is likely to be blown onto rocks and smashed to pieces on the jagged coast in long ocean swells. Treacherous reefs stretching offshore from Duxbury Point and off Point Reyes have claimed numerous vessels. The only sizable sandy areas on that rocky coast are Ten Mile Beach at Point Reyes, Drakes Bay, Stinson Beach, and Ocean Beach. Smaller beaches exist at Tennessee Cove and Rodeo Lagoon in Marin County and at Baker Beach in San Francisco. Even so, tremendous pounding from Pacific swells has demolished vessels stranded on those beaches.

No more shipping hazards lie directly in the sea lanes for twenty-five miles off the Golden Gate. The rocky Farallon Islands and their satellite Noonday Rock, twenty-six miles offshore, are major threats to vessels traveling along the coast or attempting to approach the entrance to San Francisco Bay. Another danger is a huge crescent-shaped sandbar guarding the Golden Gate. Pacific swells break on the bar's shallow waters, and ships must navigate extremely difficult wave conditions and unpredictable currents in these shoals at the harbor entrance. San Francisco Bay is vast, taking water from California's major rivers. Currents pick up speed as they pass through the narrow harbor entrance. Counter currents and back eddies in the coves and bights on each side of the main channel create especially dangerous conditions.

Heavy maritime traffic and the natural hazards led to many shipwrecks. One of the first concerns of the Federal and state government was to erect aids to navigation and life-saving stations to assist shipwreck victims. The first lighthouse built by the United States on the Pacific Coast blinked on Alcatraz Island just inside the harbor entrance. A lighthouse followed at Point Bonita. Mariners had lobbied a long time for a lighthouse at Point Bonita, whose dangers became

The motor lifeboat Majestic at Point Bonita. Launched by rail, the lifeboat saved many lives at the Golden Gate. Today, only the rusting rails and the foundations of the boathouse remain on the beach at Point Bonita.

more apparent with the wreck of the steamer *Tennessee* in March 1853. Since thick fog claimed the ship, Point Bonita gained the Pacific coast's first fog signal. Point Reyes, a prominent landfall for vessels sailing in from the Pacific, and Point Montara, south of the Golden Gate on the San Mateo shore, both received lighthouses, as did the rocky Farallon Islands. After the disastrous loss of the steamer *City of Rio de Janeiro* in 1901, the United States Lighthouse Establishment erected a light atop the dangerous, surf-washed Mile Rocks, commonly believed to be the cause of the wreck. Other submerged rocks were blasted away.

Even with lighthouses and fog signals, ships continued to wreck. The rendering of assistance to shipwrecked mariners dates to Colonial times, but it was not until the 1850s that humanitarian groups built regular stations for assistance on isolated shores where ships repeatedly wrecked. These stations became manned outposts under the control of the federal government just before the Civil War. The young United States Life-Saving Service expanded in the 1870s and 1880s, building life-saving stations on the Pacific coast. In 1879 the first station was built on Ocean Beach below the Cliff House at the foot of Fulton Street. Other stations closely followed at the Golden Gate, one in 1887 just past Fort Point, another at the southern end of Ocean Beach. Ships often crashed on the northern head of Point Bonita, so the Point Bonita Life-Saving Station was established in 1886. Farther north, Point Reyes was the site of a life-saving station in 1888 at Ten Mile Beach that was moved to Drakes Bay in 1927. A life-saving station was also constructed on the shores of Bolinas Lagoon in 1881, but the wooden boathouse burned to the ground in 1885. The tragic loss of life when the steam schooner *Hanalei* ran aground in 1914 resulted in a quick appropriation of funds in February 1915 by Congress for construction of a station at Bolinas the same year. *Hanalei* was the last major wreck on Duxbury Reef, however, and the new station was never fully put to the test. It was abandoned in 1946.

The Life-Saving Service became part of the U.S. Coast Guard in 1915, and in 1939 the Lighthouse Service merged with the Coast Guard, which gradually decommissioned and closed the life-saving stations as San Francisco declined as a port. Although greatly diminished, the life-savers are still vitally necessary. There are dozens of boating accidents each year. Capsized yachts and recreational boating emergencies, fishing boats gone ashore, and an occasional tanker or freighter now form the core of the shipwrecks at the Golden Gate. Even with modern technology and ready assistance, maritime disasters still happen.

The Fort Point Lifesaving Station, just inside the Golden Gate, remained in service until 1989. A new Coast Guard Station at Fort Baker replaced the century old-lifesaving station in 1989.

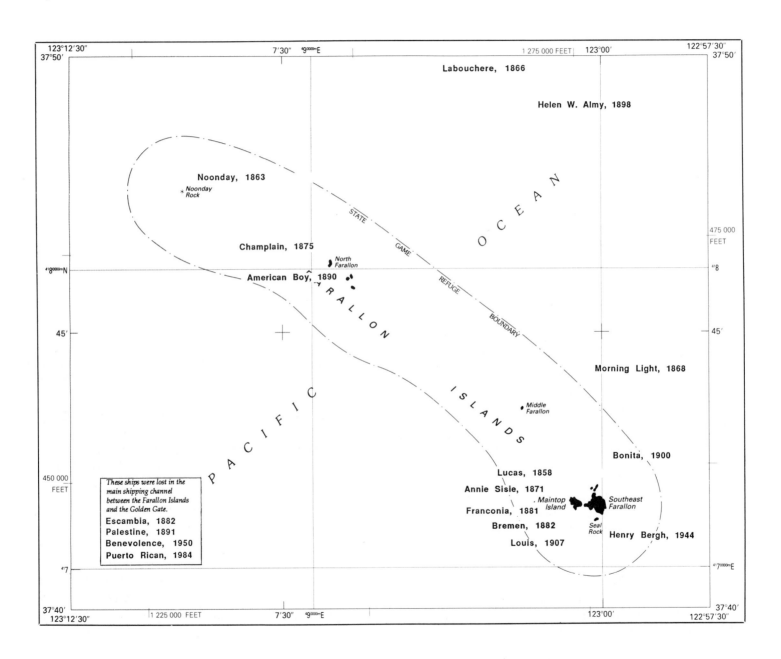

Chapter 1
Wrecks Of The Farallon Islands And The Main Ship Channel

The rocky Farallon Islands lying twenty-six miles off the Golden Gate dominate the outer approaches to San Francisco Bay. These outcroppings, the drowned peaks of a pre-Ice Age coastal range, thrust upward directly in the sea lanes, threatening vessels traveling along the coast or attempting to enter the bay. Dozens of ships have come to grief on the Farallones' rocky shores. Many have stranded but escaped with little or no damage. The tremendous discharge of the bay has created a massive sand bar curving three miles out from Ocean Beach before it sweeps toward shore and ends in the shoal waters of the Potato Patch, which received its name from capsized cargoes of potatoes swept off wrecked coasters carrying produce from Bolinas. The exact number of shipwrecks in the Gulf of the Farallones is a mystery, especially because many ships were lost with all hands aboard. The broken hulks of many vessels lie off the Farallones before the continental shelf ends and the bottom plunges into the abyss of the deep ocean. The first known wreck in the Farallones was the ship *Lucas* in 1858.

Lucas
November 11, 1858

Lucas was a small, bluff-bowed, full-rigged ship built on Maine's Penobscot Bay in 1828 that came to the Pacific, as did so many other vessels, with the human tide of those seeking California gold. In Pacific trade, *Lucas* was owned in partnership by Mr. Dagget and Leonidas Haskell of San Francisco. Following the California gold rush, other gold discoveries had attracted Californians to Australia and British Columbia, where a rich strike on the Fraser River heralded the Alaskan gold rush forty years later.

Lucas sailed from Victoria, British Columbia in the fall of 1858 with 180 passengers on board, most of them gold-seekers returning disillusioned from the Fraser River. The ship had been running south in constant fog without benefit of accurate sightings for several days, when it struck a rock in the dead of night on November 11, 1858 and broached to as the ocean swells hit. The crew attempted to free the vessel by kedging the anchor, with no success. People abandoned ship by small boat, by swimming, or by ropes brought a "few hundred yards" to shore by swimmers, as the "crew worked nobly to save the passengers."

Within an hour of running on the rocks, only the topsail yards of *Lucas* were visible. Dawn revealed the ship had run upon "Seal Rock," to the "southward and eastward of the main Farallon Island, distant about 300 yards." The keepers of the newly established Farallon Island Lighthouse worked hard to care for the survivors, until the U.S. Survey Steamer *Active* was dispatched to pick them up. Between fifteen and thirty people lost their lives. The *Alta California* reported,

"As near as we can learn, this is the first vessel lost on these islands."

A reporter from the *Alta California* described the wreck scene the next day:

Between Seal Rock and the main island . . . lay a dark mass . . . composed of sticks & timbers, black coils of rigging, blocks, deadeyes, painted posts, crosstrees, shivered yards . . . while occasionally a long, smooth, rounded, skow-like object floated up and sank again almost as instantly, and so continued re-appearing and vanishing. This was the bottom of the wrecked Lucas *the only single object pertaining to which that was not in a damaged or ruined condition was a large anchor, the stock of which projected on the sunken bows above the balance of the wreck.*

Noonday
January 1, 1863

Noonday was an elegant medium clipper ship built in New England for the California trade. On its maiden voyage, *Noonday* sailed under the command of William Blacker Gerry from Boston to San Francisco. Clearing Boston on October 17, 1855, *Noonday* arrived at San Francisco 139 days later. The clipper made three additional voyages between San Francisco and Boston, via Calcutta and Batavia, where it was repaired after striking a rock near the Banda Islands. *Noonday* was lost on the fourth passage, 139 days out of Boston on January 1, 1863. Under full sail and making nine to ten knots off the Farallones, the ship suddenly struck a submerged rock hidden by the deep ocean swells. *Noonday* continued on, but the hull planks were smashed in. The ship began to sink even as the captain pressed onward for the pilot boat *Relief*, two miles distant. *Noonday* soon settled in the water, and Capt. Henry and the crew took to the boats. The ship filled so quickly that the crew had time to rescue only a few personal effects before *Noonday* sank in 240 feet of water.

The pilotboat picked the crew, but saved nothing from the ship. General merchandise valued at $450,000 sank beneath the waves. The rock *Noonday* had struck, hitherto uncharted and eighteen feet deep, was named "Noonday Rock." In spite of the depth, salvors attempted to remove the cargo, in some reports valued as high at $600,000. The steamer *Active* sailed from San Francisco on January 3, 1863, with the intent of grappling for the hulk and attaching hawsers. The results of that attempt are unknown. *Noonday's* bell was recovered when the trawler *Junto* dragged a net across the wreck site while fishing near the Farallones in April 1934.

The wreck of *Noonday* spurred preventive measures, as the *Marysville Daily Appeal* noted:

> *The United States schooner* William L. Marcy *arrived in port last evening, having been absent since the 26th inst. in search of the mysterious* Fanny Shoal, *which was found and located by the officers who had the* Marcy *in charge . . . the Department at Washington will be immediately telegraphed to in regard to the survey of the shoal, after which will be published an account of the survey, when the correct bearings, distance, soundings and all other particulars will be given that will be of service in preventing another* Noonday *disaster and the loss of any more $400,000 cargoes!*

Labouchere
April 15, 1866

Labouchere was a wooden-hulled steamer built either in London or the Clyde River area of Scotland in 1858. The 160-horsepower steam engine was thought to be "very superior, being built for the Great Exhibition in London in 1851, at which they took the highest prize." Prize-winning engines notwithstanding, *Labouchere* was considered to be "of small size and a slow traveller." The steamer began its service with the Hudson's Bay Company under Capt. J. Trivett, with London as home port. Before the end of the decade, however, the steamer was dispatched to the Pacific and entered into the coastal passenger trade linking British Columbia, Oregon, and California.

Beginning late in 1865 or early in 1866, *Labouchere* made its first voyage between British Columbia and San Francisco. The second voyage on the run ended in disaster. Under the command of Capt. W.A. Mouat, *Labouchere* stood away from the Howard Street Wharf on the evening of April 14, 1866, with approximately one hundred passengers and a full load of general cargo consigned to Falkner, Bell & Co. on board. In calm but foggy weather, the ship steamed north at nine knots until Point Reyes was sighted. The point's rocky headlands loomed up without warning, the lookouts spotting the shore with only seconds to spare "while the breakers roared around them." The steamer struck a submerged ledge near Chimney Rock. *Labouchere* "backed off the reef into deep water, and the engines were put under full steam in order to keep the pumps — four in number — running. Unfortunately the captain did not head back to San Francisco. *Labouchere* aimlessly steamed around the open water off Point Reyes all night since Capt. Mouat thought the damage was slight and would not "necessitate the abandonment of the trip."

Early on the morning of the fifteenth, a new leak was reported. Water began to gain rapidly on the pumps. Capt. Mouat ordered the boats launched and the passengers taken ashore some eight miles distant. Some thugs on board attempted to rush the boats, but were repelled by a shot from the captain's revolver. Crew members launched eight boats, but one was upset by the ship's gangway and two men were

The "hell-ship" Bremen, *wrecked on South Farallon Island, October 16, 1882.*

drowned. Fortunately for the twenty-three still on board, the Italian fishing smack *Andrew* hove into sight and took all hands off just before *Labouchere* made a final plunge. Soon all that was left in sight was the deck cabin, recently installed in San Francisco, which floated free as the vessel went down. All survivors in boats made shore, and were cared for at the ranch of Mr. Flood and family near Point Reyes, until the tug *Rescue* came from San Francisco to pick them up. The wreck of *Labouchere* has never been located. A trawler working off Point Reyes a few years ago caught a pressed brick of coal with the mark of a crown pressed into its face that may have come from the ill-fated British steamer.

Morning Light
January 18, 1868

The two-masted, forty-three-ton schooner *Morning Light* of San Francisco was built in 1858 by Henry B. Tichenor at his South Beach yard on San Francisco Bay. A New York wholesale commission merchant, Tichenor came to California in April 1850 and established himself in business in partnership with Firman Neefus, who managed the New York end of their affairs. From wholesale commission sales Tichenor branched out into shipbuilding and coastal shipping, particularly the lumber trade. He established the first marine railway on the Pacific Coast in 1851 at the foot of Second Street in San Francisco. Tichenor was one of San Francisco's more successful and influential maritime merchants, in large part because of his diverse interests and activities. He constructed

Morning Light to use in the coastal lumber trade, and the schooner sailed for a decade before its fateful end.

Details of the wreck are scarce. Under the command of Captain Stevens, *Morning Light* was bound south from the Russian River in January 1868 with fifty thousand feet of lumber consigned to Tichenor & Co. The weather was foul, and the newspapers reported that it was the "roughest storm in many years." The schooner sprung a leak and filled with water, and the crew took to a boat. Tossed on heavy seas, the boat made South Farallon Island, where the crew was rescued by the lighthouse keepers. Southeast winds drove the water-logged schooner ashore on North Farallon Island. *Morning Light* was a total loss.

Annie Sisie
September 18, 1871

G. Raynes at Portsmouth, New Hampshire built the full-rigged ship *Annie Sisie* in 1856, in the last full flush of pre-Civil War American shipbuilding. *Sisie* was a vessel of quality, built of the stoutest white oak, fastened strongly with copper and iron. No sleek clipper, but rather a bluff-bowed trader, the vessel was designed to carry a full load of general cargo for its owners, Sisie & Chase, of Portsmouth. On its last voyage, *Annie Sisie*'s cargo was said to be railroad iron and coal for the Central Pacific R.R. The ship went ashore on South Farallon Island on September 18, 1871. Captain Tucker must have "lost his way reckoning completely," for he ran the ship on a reef off the west end of South Farallon Island with all sails set and anchors hanging by the shank painters. Contemporary reference to "a mystery overhangs the disaster" indicates that some criticism of the captain must have been made, but was never made public. Dense fog probably caused the wreck.

Island residents found the ship's log book and chronometer boxes, but the chronometer was missing and the cabin had been "well cleared out." *Annie Sisie* was not salvaged, and in the open Pacific swells rapidly went to pieces. About September 27, the wreck was sold to the Pacific Wrecking Company for $500, the small price indicating little of value could be recovered from the shattered hulk. Presumably the wreck's owners tried to recoup their investment, but their results are unknown.

Champlain
June 17, 1875

Champlain was a New England-built "downeaster" with a brief career. As large, full-bodied wooden ships usually built in Maine, downeasters were the typical American deepwater sailers of the last decades of the nineteenth century. On *Champlain*'s maiden voyage to Bombay, India, the ship's passage was fast enough to set a record. From Bombay, the downeaster sailed to Madras and thence New York, taking in a general cargo for San Francisco. Departing New York on February 15, 1875 in company with five other fast ships, *Champlain* could have beat them all into the Golden Gate by as much as forty days—but went ashore

on the Farallones on June 17.

Nearing San Francisco 121 days out of New York, *Champlain* entered a dense fog bank. For two days the pea soup held, when "the lookout uttered the fearful cry of breakers ahead." After the ship struck, the captain ordered the crew to take to the boats, as the vessel slid off the rocks and began to settle rapidly. Capt. Reuben Merril and sixteen others piled into a longboat and began to pull away. As they rowed under the ship's bow, a swell lifted the boat just as the ship's bow came down. With crashing impact the bowsprit struck and the martingale stay impaled the boat, killing the captain and mortally wounding a seaman. The schooner *Mendocino* picked up the shocked and struggling survivors.

The ship's cargo, fully insured, was itemized in great detail, and reads like an encyclopedia of deepwater trade:

> *Ash, boxes, bottles & jars, bolts, boots & shoes, bitters, copra, chairs, cork fenders, coal, candles, cocoa mats, crucibles, earthenware, emery, galvanized iron pipe, gas fixtures, glassware, iron pipe, iron, ink, tobacco, marble, nails, oil cloth, oak plank, paper hangings, pipe staves, pitch, paper, peppers, pumps, rosin, stoves, starch, spikes, tin, tar, trunks, tiles, whiskey and wine.*

Such a potentially rich wreck was sold in short order for $500 to N. Bruns of San Francisco. The low price clearly indicated the paltry chances for profit, since Bruns' "first and principal job [was] to find her." Speculation ran that *Champlain* "has gone to the

Palestine *was a total loss on the San Francisco Bar.*

bottom of the sea." The search by the tug *Neptune* was unpleasant for those on board, and seasickness of the would-be salvors was described in delightfully tongue-in-cheek fashion. "One was so disgusted that he immediately made his will on his return, and another who thought he saw the ship [beneath the water] with a main spenser set, was sufficiently excited by a spirit of true inwardness to offer up all of his effects to the god who rules the briny deep. Both have since recovered, and are again useful members of society." Bruns lost his $500 gamble. The wreck of *Champlain* was not found, and to this day its whereabouts are a mystery.

Franconia
June 27, 1881

The downeaster *Franconia* was "of full model" and staunchly built. The ship was laid down in 1874 in the famous shipbuilding center of Bath, Maine. The builders, William V. Moses & Sons, prominent Bath shipbuilders, had launched many vessels in the three decades since they first opened their yard in 1842. *Franconia*, a typical deepwater trader, was engaged for seven years as "a general trader to South America, India and the ports of the far east," when wrecked at the Farallon Islands on its first passage to San Francisco. Capt. William H. Otis commanded the vessel since at least 1876, and his familiarity with Golden Gate waters dated to the gold rush, when he had called at San Francisco as master of the ship *Rome*.

As *Franconia* approached the Golden Gate in a thick fog, the captain's experience availed him little. By dead reckoning the ship should have been off Point Reyes, but struck Middle Rock without warning. Lookouts belatedly spotted land on all sides. *Franconia* had run ashore on South Farallon Island within a stone's throw of the fog signal. Within fifteen minutes the ship lay "hard and fast on a sandy beach in a bight on the northwest side of the island." The captain, his wife, the entire crew of twenty-one, and all their effects landed at the Farallon Island Light Station and removed to San Francisco the next day.

The wreck was blamed on the fog whistle, unheard before or after the accident. The nature of *Franconia*'s cargo was unspecified, but records indicate the value to be $250,000. Reports sent to San Francisco said, "Nothing can be done to save the ship and she has started to break up . . . and portions of her cargo were going ashore. . . " The next day, newspapers reported that the ship's sails, rigging, and spars would be salvaged, and that "the purchaser can, without doubt, if he works to advantage, make a good and quick turn on his investment."

Escambia
June 19, 1882

The iron-hulled screw steamer *Escambia* was built at Sunderland, Great Britain in 1879 for the Escambia Steamship Co., Ltd. of Liverpool. The 1,401-ton steamer was sent to the Orient, and from there carried Chinese workers from Hong Kong to Victoria, British Columbia. Loading coal at Departure Bay, the ship steamed to San Francisco and discharged its cargo in exchange for 2,350 tons of wheat. According to the *Daily Alta California*, *Escambia* was poorly loaded with eighty tons of coal stacked on the deck and the ballast tanks pumped empty.

Steaming out to sea late in the afternoon on June 19, 1882, the steamer listed and "rolled down until her plank sheer was in the water." Capt. John Low at the Point Lobos Marine Exchange Lookout watched *Escambia* discharge the pilot and head for the bar "almost on her beam ends." A half-mile from the bar, the top-heavy vessel capsized. Rushing to abandon ship, a panicked sailor overturned a lifeboat and the smallest boat aboard was the only one to pull free of the sinking steamer. Capt. Purvis, the engineer, steward, cook, and three seamen pulled for the beach, where surf capsized the boat. The three sailors drowned, and the captain, engineer, steward, and cook were the only survivors of the disaster.

The wreck was found by rescuers in five and one-half fathoms of water off the bar and was blasted to clear the channel. Despite reports of faulty loading, a court of inquiry exonerated Capt. Purvis. The British Consul ruled that the engines had eased off at a dangerous moment, the vessel fell broadside into the waves, and the opposing pressure of wind and the strong ebb tide had tipped *Escambia* over.

Bremen

October 16, 1882

Mutiny, sickness, and starvation is the legacy of the notorious *Bremen*. Built as an iron-hulled steamship in Scotland in 1858, the ship plied the trans-Atlantic route between Bremen and New York for a dozen years until the coal-burning engines were removed.

Fitted out as a sailing vessel and re-rigged as a ship, *Bremen* commenced a new career flying the red ensign of the British merchant marine alongside the house flag of E. Bates & Sons of Liverpool.

Bremen's two recorded voyages from Liverpool to San Francisco carried full cargoes of coal. Both voyages arrived at San Francisco after harvest time, and California grain was probably the return cargo. *Bremen*'s notoriety began when the vessel arrived in San Francisco in 1875 after a hellish voyage with a crew more dead than alive. On February 6, 1875, *Bremen* had cleared Liverpool with captain, three mates, carpenter, carpenter's mate, three apprentices, one able-bodied seaman, thirty-six "colored" seamen, and two stowaway boys. One stowaway was the captain's son, who was running away from home.

Six days out, Charles Purvey, one of the black seamen, reported sick. He was sick indeed, for an examination showed that his "lungs were completely gone." Although the captain treated him with "cough pills" from the ship's medicine chest, Purvey died. Despite rations of lime juice, sickness increased among the crew until, in superstitious panic, one watch "in open revolt" refused to work, and their ringleader threatened to "cut the mate's lip off." Threats and an armed captain restored discipline. Two men were put in irons for a week on bread and water.

The black seamen, born in the tropical regions of the British Empire, became demoralized as the passage grew colder and the vessel headed south into the violent seas 'round Cape Horn. In panic, they refused treatment of lime juice, turnips, and the fresh foods that would have saved them. Symptoms of scurvy appeared, despite the cook's offerings of sago,

Helen W. Almy *sailed with eager goldseekers for Alaska in 1898; everyone on board perished when the bark capsized in heavy seas on the San Francisco Bar.*

rice, arrowroot, oatmeal, and fresh meat twice a week. All told, thirteen men died on the gruesome 121-day passage to San Francisco. On arrival, *Bremen* was christened a "floating coffin" by the local press.

Seven years later under Capt. Dougal, *Bremen* was approaching San Francisco in a heavy fog, 118 days out from Liverpool. After midnight on October 16, 1882, as the captain prepared to give the order to heave to and wait for better visibility, the cry of "breakers" and "land" was heard from the lookout. The ship's bow crashed on the northwest side of South Farallon Island, the stern sank, and the vessel struck heavily in a severe swell. All hands were saved as the ship was abandoned. *Bremen* went ashore within a short distance of where *Franconia* had been lost in similar circumstances. Reports of both wrecks indicated that the whistle of the Farallon Island Light Station's fog signal was never heard, and the two ships had crashed ashore practically beneath it. Capt. Dougal of *Bremen*, hanging from the jibboom, managed to leap ashore onto the rocks near the fog signal. According to a reminiscent account published in the San Francisco *Call* in January 1898, "It was at this moment that the attendant of the fog signal apparatus was about to blow a warning. . . . Just as the man was about to sound the fog signal the captain of the wrecked ship appeared on a huge rock in front of the station, [and] frightened the keeper almost to death. 'You needn't blow the thing now,' shouted the almost exhausted captain. 'It's all over with the *Bremen*.' "

American Boy
November 4, 1890

American Boy was a two-masted schooner of 183 tons, made of Douglas fir and fastened with iron and copper. Built in 1882 by Hiram Doncaster at Seabeck, in what was then called "Washington Territory," *American Boy* was home ported in San Francisco, where its owners used the schooner for shipping lumber. Its career seems to be typical of most schooners in the lumber trade, and when surveyed in San Francisco in 1885 and 1886 for the American Bureau of Shipping, *American Boy* was noted to be in excellent condition. *American Boy* wrecked on the foggy morning of November 4, 1890 while sailing south from Grays Harbor, Washington, loaded with lumber. Ploughing ashore on the North Farallones, the vessel and cargo were a total loss, but the men aboard were all able to take to the ship's boat and were later picked up by a tug.

Palestine
June 27, 1891

The 1,397-ton downeaster *Palestine* was constructed in 1877 by W.V. Moses & Son at Bath, Maine on the builder's own account, and sailed in the Cape Horn trade to San Francisco. The ship made a single voyage to Singapore in 1880. Sold to Samuel Blair, the vessel was employed as a collier between Puget Sound and San Francisco and made twenty-two voyages before wrecking. While crossing the bar on June 27, 1891,

Palestine struck and filled with water. Tugs raced to save the ship but could not budge it since the vessel was heavily laden with tons of coal. The crew was saved and the ship abandoned. Soon only the topmasts protruded from the water, marking the wreck until it broke up.

Helen W. Almy
March 20, 1898

The loss of the bark *Helen W. Almy* was doubly tragic. Attended with dreadful loss of life, it is one of the region's least-known maritime disasters, because there were no survivors and no evidence cast ashore to tell the tale. *Helen W. Almy* was launched in Connecticut in 1859, and soon brought to California. There sea captains bought the bark to trade between Hawaii and San Francisco. By 1863 *Almy* provided regular service for freight and passengers to the Pacific Northwest with the California and Oregon Packet Line. In 1861 an active coastal trade between Oregon and California resumed after a few years of idleness. Several barks regularly sailed between Portland and San Francisco in the 1860s, including *Helen W. Almy*. Between 1862 and 1863, this fleet of Oregon packets entered the Columbia River fifty-five times.

After its active career, when "the bark was the equal of any similar vessel on the Coast," *Helen W. Almy* was sold to McCollam Fishing and Trading Company. At Puget Sound McCollam refitted the bark for codfishing and later for the lumber trade. The aging *Almy* was sent again to the South Seas, where the bark was dismasted in a storm. Sent back to California and laid up in Oakland Creek, *Almy* was doomed to eventual deterioration. Briefly taken out, *Almy* took part in an aborted "blackbirding" scheme to carry natives of the Gilbert Islands as indentured laborers to Mexico.

Greed and the lure of gold in the Klondike in 1898 induced the owners to pull *Helen W. Almy* off the mudflats to be fitted for sea. By now the vessel had been cut down to a barkentine, or double-topmast schooner. A group of speculators took the ship over and fitted it to take gold-seekers to Alaska's Copper River, via Seattle. Passage was cheap in the unseaworthy vessel, but since the passengers were out-of-towners, no questions were asked about the ship's condition. Crewmembers were found only by scrounging the waterfront for the dregs of the boarding houses because many sailors refused to ship aboard the antiquated *Almy*. The ill-fated, badly manned vessel was towed to sea on Sunday morning, March 20, 1898 by the tug *Sea Witch* into heavy swells and a stiff northwest breeze. A storm brewed outside the Gate.

Helen W. Almy was found floating capsized and abandoned five miles off the San Francisco shore the following day by the steamer *Santa Rosa*. Probably the ship had capsized the night it left port. The hulk lay on its starboard side, which indicated to the experienced seamen on rescue tugs that *Almy* was headed home when disaster struck. There was no one left to rescue. All thirty-nine aboard had perished without a trace, and the battered, worthless hulk was allowed to drift away. Three causes were determined: the old vessel was unfit for sea, the crew was not fit for duty, and the vessel floated too high and was improperly ballasted. More than twenty years later, the fishing trawler *Ituna* snagged its nets on a wreck in forty-seven fathoms of water "at a point nearly midway between Point Reyes and the North Farralon island." *Ituna's* captain believed the wreck was *Helen W. Almy.*

Bonita
July 21, 1900

The pilot schooner *Bonita*, built at Port Blakely, Washington in 1892, was constructed to cruise off the San Francisco bar and hail incoming ships seeking a pilot to guide them in. On the evening of July 21, 1900 the schooner was lying six miles off the Farallones. Surrounded by whales, the hapless vessel was rammed on the port quarter, splitting open the hull. Filling with water, *Bonita* was abandoned and sank in four hours. Capt. Scott and pilots Wallace, Miller, and Swanson were rescued by the pilot schooner *Gracie S.*

Louis
June 19, 1907

Louis was an unusual vessel with an interesting history. Built at North Bend, Oregon in 1888 by John Kruse, it was laid down as a steamer but rigged as a schooner with five temporary masts, then sailed south to San Francisco for installation of engines. She thus became the first ocean-going five-masted schooner. The temporary rig performed so well, however, that

the engines were never put in. Two masts were stepped off-center to give greater spread of sail while running before the wind.

The Simpson Lumber Company of San Francisco owned *Louis* throughout its career, which was largely spent hauling lumber from the Northwest. In November 1902 the schooner left South Bend, Washington bound for East London, South Africa. Reaching that port seven months and a day later, *Louis* continued east to Newcastle, Australia, and Lahaina, Hawaii, finally arriving back in South Bend in October 1903 — the first time a five-masted schooner had circled the globe.

Subsequent coastal passages took *Louis* as far north as the Aleutian Islands and as far south as Redondo, California. Twice the ship brushed with disaster. The schooner struck on the bar while being towed out of Willapa, Washington harbor in 1904, causing a steady leak throughout the voyage. Two years later, while being towed into San Francisco, *Louis* collided with the British ship *Clan Galbraith.* The jiggermast was carried away, the cabin stove in, and bulwarks, rail, and starboard side badly damaged. By then the heavily used vessel was much the worse for wear. The story is told that the crew, rather than washing the schooner down "fore and aft," were ordered to begin amidships and work towards both ends — in other words, the vessel was so badly hogged that it had lost all sheer, and the water would no longer run to the midships scuppers.

Louis' final voyage started at Gray's Harbor, Washington, bound for San Francisco with nine hundred thousand board feet of railroad ties. The ship never arrived, wrecking on South Farallon Island on

The *five-masted schooner* Louis, *a rare type of vessel on the Pacific coast, was lost at the west end of South Farallon Island, close to where the ships* Franconia *and* Bremen *had previously been lost.*

June 19, 1907. Surfmen of the United States Life-Saving Service who were on the scene described the disaster:

Stranded at 2:30 a.m. in dense fog, about 30 miles WSW of stations. Moderately rough sea. Reported by Merchant's Exchange and by Weather Bureau. Both (lifesaving) crews (Fort Point and Point Bonita) were immediately mustered for service, and upon arrival of the tug Sea Queen *they were taken in tow for the Farralon Islands, where the wreck had occurred. The schooner was found fast ashore, full of water, and in danger of going to pieces at any moment. The master refused to leave her, so the lifesavers rigged up a breeches buoy between her and the island. By evening the sea had made up so that the master was persuaded to leave; 5 were taken ashore in the breeches buoy and 5 in the ship's boat. The surfboat crews were then towed back to port. The schooner went to pieces that night.*

Louis went to pieces at Franconia Beach, where the ships *Franconia* and *Bremen* were wrecked on the northwest side of South Farallon Island.

Henry Bergh
May 31, 1944

Henry Bergh was a liberty ship owned by the War Shipping Administration. Operated by the Norton Lilly Company and chartered to the U.S. Navy, *Bergh* was one of thirty-three selected from the thousands of liberties for use as a troopship, and was officially rated to carry 564 passengers plus crew and a naval armed guard. *Henry Bergh* was built in the famous mass-production shipyards established by Henry J. Kaiser on marshland in Richmond, California. Launched in June 1943, by the following February *Henry Bergh* was at San Francisco, shuttling between there and the South Pacific.

On its final voyage, *Henry Bergh* was bound to San Francisco from Pearl Harbor, overloaded with thirteen hundred sailors returning from the war and a crew of nearly a hundred. Before dawn on May 31, 1944, the ship steamed through thick fog for thirty-six hours without an opportunity to take a navigational fix. Unknown to Capt. Joseph C. Chambers, his allowances for current and wind were in error. *Bergh* had set to the north by nearly ten miles, and was heading straight for South Farallon Island at a full speed of eleven knots. A whistle, faintly heard over the raucous celebrations of veterans returning home, was wrongly assumed to be a passing ship, and the vessel continued on. Five minutes later a faint whistle was heard again, and almost immediately land was spotted dead ahead. Despite prompt evasive action, *Henry Bergh* ran hard aground on jagged rocks about two hundred yards offshore at 5:00 a.m. The engines, straining full astern, could not budge the ship.

Although *Henry Bergh*'s SOS reached San Francisco at 5:05 a.m. and help was immediately dispatched, none would arrive for hours, and the captain ordered the ship abandoned. The weather was fairly calm, the abandonment "so orderly it was more like a drill." One veteran later remarked, "after what we went through in the war. . . this morning was mild." The troops were shuttled ashore twenty-five at a time in eight lifeboats, by breeches buoy rigged between wreck and shore, and by swimming. When the first rescue craft arrived at 8:00 a.m., six hundred men had safely landed. By early afternoon, all hands were safely aboard other ships, despite the pounding surf, cold water, and treacherous currents. A volunteer crew remained on board as a tug passed heavy hawsers aboard and tried to haul *Henry Bergh* off the rocks, but the hull cracked at the No. 4 hatch, and it became clear that it was beyond salvage. As the captain — the last man aboard — left, *Henry Bergh* began to go to pieces. The rescue of every man on board *Henry Bergh* was a remarkable achievement; only two men were injured and thirty-five required hospitalization for exposure. But for luck and good discipline, the toll might have been much greater.

In the wreck's aftermath, the Coast Guard held an investigation. Capt. Chambers made errors in plotting his vessel's course, proceeding at an unsafe speed through the thick fog, and failing to use navigational aids including taking soundings. He also permitted his passengers to be so noisy as to interfere with the hearing of his lookouts. He was demoted to the rank of first mate. Photographic evidence indicates that *Henry Bergh* rapidly broke into three sections. The hull forward of the bridge was hard ashore on South Farallon the day following the wreck, while the stern and the bridge sections lay partially submerged, the bridge just offshore, and the stern hung up on a reef about two hundred yards away. No salvage was attempted, and *Henry Bergh*'s battered remains still lie off the island.

Benevolence
August 25, 1950

It is ironic that a vessel whose purpose was to provide aid for the sick and wounded became the victim in one of the greatest maritime disasters off the Golden Gate. *Benevolence* was a Navy hospital ship converted from a U.S. Maritime Commission standard C-4 type cargo vessel originally named *Marine Lion*. Built at the Sun Shipbuilding Company of Chester, Pa., the ship was launched on July 10, 1944. Within the month *Marine Lion* was transferred to the U.S. Navy for conversion to a hospital ship. That work was carried out at the Todd-Erie Basin Shipyard at Brooklyn, N.Y. and completed by May 12, 1945. The vessel was then commissioned into the U.S. Navy as *Benevolence* (AH-13).

Benevolence was dispatched to Eniwitok Atoll, where the crew spent weeks tending to the sick and wounded evacuated after Third Fleet operations against Japan's home islands. The ship accompanied the battle fleet for the last air strikes against the Japanese homeland, and was among the first to receive Allied prisoners of war liberated after the cease-fire. Thousands of Americans had been transported to Japan to replace laborers lost to conscription, and their return home ended the war's tragic drama. *Benevolence* shuttled three times between Pearl Harbor and the States with wounded from the Pacific. The hospital ship participated in the Operation Crossroads atomic bomb tests at Bikini Atoll in 1946, and sailed to Tsingtao, China in 1946 for the last cruise before inactivation in the fall of 1947.

The submerged hulk of the Navy hospital ship Benevolence, *its white hull visible through the water, was one of the worst shipping disasters off the Golden Gate. Eighteen people lost their lives when the freighter* Mary Luckenbach *rammed and sank the hospital ship on August 25, 1950.*

In 1950 *Benevolence*, removed from "mothballs," went to Mare Island Naval Shipyard to be refitted for service in the Korean War. During a series of routine tests outside the Golden Gate, tragedy struck. On August 25, as *Benevolence* returned and proceeded east in the main ship channel at seventeen knots, the ship entered a fog bank. Radar announced the presence of five ships, but none appeared near enough to present a hazard. Suddenly the bow of the freighter *Mary Luckenbach* loomed out of the fog. Emergency maneuvering by the hospital ship was in vain. The *Luckenbach* pierced its port side with a crash, and raked along the *Benevolence*'s hull before again holing the vessel further aft. Water poured into the gashes and spread through the ship as it ruptured the internal water-tight bulkheads. Listing to port, the hospital ship began to settle by the bow. Calls for help filled the air waves, but no order was given to abandon ship. *Benevolence* sank within forty minutes.

Benevolence had packed 526 people aboard in two crews of Navy personnel and civilians training to take over. Men and women struggled for hours in the cold water, while a fleet of forty rescue vessels combed the foggy ocean for survivors. When rescuers took a count, they realized that *Benevolence* was the worst maritime disaster since the 1901 wreck of *City of Rio de Janiero*. Eighteen people died. Three-quarters of the supplies and equipment and half a load of seagoing provisions went down with the ship. Just as Italian fishermen had saved many survivors of *Rio de Janeiro*, so another Italian fisherman was a hero when *Benevolence* sank. Throwing his cargo overboard, fisherman John Napoli pulled many oil-soaked, half-dead survivors aboard, badly wrenching his back and nearly sinking his overloaded craft, the thirty-four-foot *Flora*. Napoli saved as many as seventy lives. Quickly forgotten after the disaster, he became a national hero when San Francisco *Chronicle* reporter J. Campbell Bruce told his story in the March 1951 edition of *Reader's Digest*.

An extensive investigation disclosed some curious particulars that contributed to the disaster: *Luckenbach*'s radar was not in use at the time of the collision, despite heavy fog. Reports of the ship's speed varied from eight to sixteen knots. Capt. Leonard C. Smith of *Luckenbach* testified that he ordered his vessel to drop anchor after the collision and that he remained on location for an hour and a half, heard no distress signals, did not attempt to contact *Benevolence* by radio, and lowered no lifeboats. He had concluded "that the damage to the hospital ship was all above the water line and that she was proceeding into port."

Benevolence came to rest on its port side in seventy-four feet of water about a mile south of the main ship channel, and about two and one-half miles southwest of the Mile Rock light. The white hull with its red crosses was clearly visible at low water. Close to the shipping channel, the wreck was a distinct hazard to navigation, and in 1952 was dynamited. More than fifty feet of water now covers the shattered remains of *Benevolence*.

Puerto Rican
November 1, 1984

The story of the supertanker *Puerto Rican* proves again that modern precautions can minimize but not entirely avoid the natural hazards of seafaring. *Puerto Rican* was a modern steel tanker over six hundred feet long, displacing thirty-four thousand deadweight tons. Originally owned in trust by the Banker's Trust Company of New York, the tanker at the time of loss was operated by the Keystone Shipping Company of Philadelphia, Pennsylvania. The specialized vessel was fitted with lined tanks to carry chemicals and liquefied gasses.

Under Capt. James C. Spillane's command, *Puerto Rican* arrived in San Francisco Bay on October 25, 1984, and called at Richmond and Alameda. The tanker loaded 91,984 barrels of lubrication oil and additives, took on 8,500 barrels of bunker fuel, and left Richmond for sea shortly after midnight on October 31, bound for New Orleans. In the early morning darkness, more than eight miles off the Golden Gate, an explosion occurred as the ship was disembarking the pilot outside the San Francisco Bay entrance channel. Near the No. 6 center-independent tank, flames blew several hundred feet into the air. Several seconds later, a second severe blast followed. A huge section of deck folded back like an orange peel. The pilot and two crew members were blown into the water. The pilot boat *San Francisco* rescued pilot James S. Nolan and third mate Philip R. Lempiere, but able seaman John Peng was lost.

Damage to the vessel was fatal. Bow and stern sections twisted crazily and hull plating was torn away. *Puerto Rican* settled by the stern. Fires burned and ravaged the innards of the huge vessel. For the day following the explosion, the seas remained calm and "ideal for fire fighting and rescue efforts," but the next day brought high winds and rough seas. Coast Guard response was immediate. The burning, leaking tanker, which had drifted to within four miles of the coast, was towed seaward to minimize a potentially disastrous oil spill on the sensitive ocean shoreline and on the rich wildlife and underwater breeding grounds of the Gulf of the Farallon Islands National Marine Sanctuary. The Oakland Fire Department also responded, sending the fireboat *City of Oakland* out past the Gate to combat the flames aboard *Puerto Rican*.

By November 2, all fires aboard were extinguished, but the next day, weakened by explosion and fire, *Puerto Rican* broke in two sections, spilling thirty thousand barrels of oil into the water. The stern sank with eighty-five hundred barrels of fuel oil fifteen miles due south of South Farallon Island and came to rest, canted at an angle, at a depth of 1,476 feet. Oil still leaks slowly from the vessel. For over a week, an intensive cleanup program worked to minimize the environmental effects of the spill, but only fifteen hundred barrels of oil were skimmed from the ocean surface. Spilled oil fouled the Farallones and the coast of Bodega Bay. More than five thousand sea birds died from the oil, but the disaster could have been even greater if not for the Herculean efforts and cooperation of various government agencies, corporate bodies, volunteer groups, and concerned citizens. On November 18, the surviving forward section of *Puerto Rican* went to Triple-A Shipyard's San Francisco dry dock for cargo removal. The derelict sailed for Taiwan on April 6, 1985, where the remains of *Puerto Rican* ended in a scrapyard.

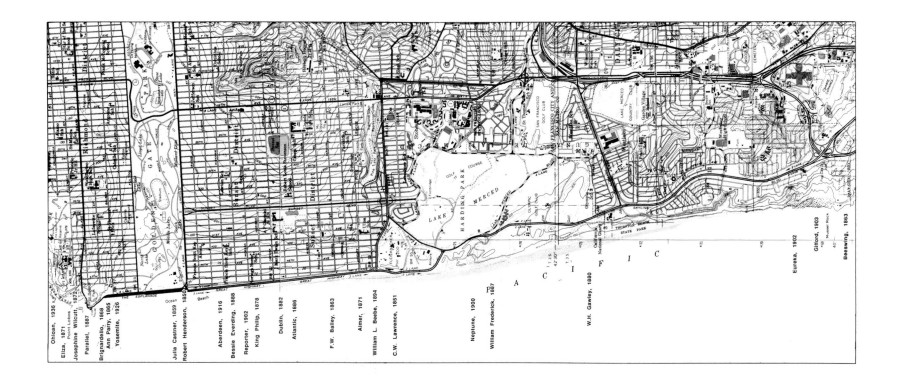

Ohioan, 1936
Eliza, 1871
Josephine Wilcutt, 1872
Parallel, 1887
Brignardello, 1868
Ann Parry, 1865
Yosemite, 1926
Julia Castner, 1859
Robert Henderson, 1850
Aberdeen, 1916
Bessie Everding, 1888
Reporter, 1902
King Philip, 1878
Dublin, 1882
Atlantic, 1886
F.W. Bailey, 1863
Almer, 1871
William L. Beebe, 1894
C.W. Lawrence, 1851
Neptune, 1900
William Frederick, 1887
W.H. Gawley, 1880
Eureka, 1902
Gifford, 1903
Beeswing, 1863

Chapter 2
Wrecks On Ocean Beach

Bordered to the north by Point Lobos and the Cliff House and to the south by Mussel Rock, San Francisco's Ocean Beach stretches for nearly seven miles to form the city's western boundary. There, west of the Golden Gate, the city's shore sweeps past the rock-bound headlands to dip into a broad expanse of sand dunes and flat beaches. The San Francisco Bar, curving from its apex three miles out, touches shore one and one-half miles south of Point Lobos, near the intersection of today's Noriega Street and the Great Highway. The flat expanse of sand and the bar's deflection of water toward shore create a surf zone of white, frothy foam and huge waves that writer Bret Harte likened to ravenous wolves racing up to meet the sand dunes.

The seven-mile stretch of beach between Point Lobos and Mussel Rock holds one of the highest concentrations of shipwrecks. More than fifty maritime accidents occurred there; twenty-four vessels and sixty-six lives were lost between 1850 and 1936. The first identified vessel was *Robert Henderson* in 1850, followed by the revenue cutter *C.W. Lawrence* in 1851. In 1859 the bark *Julia Castner* went ashore, and its timbers built a famed San Francisco institution, the Seal Rock House, which would later inspire a lasting

city landmark, the Cliff House. After the three 1850s wrecks, no other vessel wrecked until 1863, when *F.W. Bailey* and *Beeswing* were battered to pieces on the beach. The 1860s and 1870s saw more wrecks, with six in the 1880s. There was one wreck in the 1890s, *W.L. Beebe*, and four just after the turn of the century. Then, every ten years, another vessel was wrecked — in 1916, 1926, and 1936.

Robert Henderson
June 12, 1850

The first vessel wrecked on Ocean Beach was the 368-ton bark *Robert Henderson*. Built at Sunderland, Great Britain in 1838, the bark traded between Liverpool and Batavia (Java) from 1839 to 1843, when it began sailing between Liverpool and Calcutta, continuing until 1849. In the 1850s, a flood tide of emigration from the British Isles to Australia commenced, peaking in the mid-1850s. Liverpool, previously overshadowed by London as an emigration port, boomed with the "Australian Trade." A number of Liverpool-registered vessels entered in the trade, including *Robert Henderson*. In

1850 the bark sailed to Adelaide, Australia, where 165 passengers boarded for a voyage to San Francisco. The Australian response to the California gold discovery was tremendous. Dozens of vessels carried argonauts to San Francisco through the 1850s. After the 1852 gold discovery in Australia, many more ships brought hordes of gold seekers "down under" from both the United States and Great Britain.

After a 123-day passage across the Pacific via Tahiti, *Robert Henderson* arrived off the Golden Gate. The bark ran aground on one of the Farallon Islands, but was undamaged and got off. On June 23, 1850, *Robert Henderson* sailed through the Golden Gate and safely landed passengers at San Francisco. After a short stay of three weeks, the bark cleared San Francisco on Thursday, June 12, 1850 for Adelaide. The bark missed stays off Point Lobos, however, and was blown ashore "on the south [Ocean] beach." To "go in stays" meant to alter the course of the vessel when sailing against the wind, so that "she will return in the direction whence she came." Passengers and crew survived, but *Robert Henderson* was a total loss. An auctioneer sold the wreck for $170, the small sum indicating that not much of value could be gained from the bark's remains.

Cornelius W. Lawrence
November 25, 1851

The 144-ton revenue cutter *Cornelius W. Lawrence* was built by William Easby at Washington, D.C. in 1848. One of seven new cutters ordered by the United States Revenue Marine, *Lawrence* was launched on

August 20, 1848. The new cutter, rigged as a brig, was armed with five cannons, two 32-pdr. guns, two 6-pdrs., and one 18-pdr. that was later removed. *Lawrence*, commanded by Capt. Alexander Fraser, former commandant of the Revenue Marine, was sent to the Pacific to be the first Revenue Marine cutter in California, extending American customs and revenue laws to the recently acquired territory.

Lawrence sailed from Hampton Roads, Virginia on October 15, 1848 for California. After a long voyage by way of Cape Horn with stops at Rio de Janeiro, Valparaiso, and Honolulu, *Lawrence* arrived at San Francisco on October 31, 1849. At that time, the formerly small town was blossoming as thousands of gold-seekers arrived to make their fortunes. Nearly five hundred vessels lay at anchor off San Francisco, many without crews. Desertion, mutiny, and smuggling were major problems, and *Lawrence* and its crew were pressed into duty immediately. For over a year *Lawrence* remained at anchor off San Francisco, enforcing the laws of the United States. Beginning in December 1850 *Lawrence* began patrolling the California coast to search for smugglers. During the next year the brig sailed to San Diego, the California Channel Islands, Monterey, San Luis Obispo, Santa Cruz, and Hilo, Hawaii. In June 1851 Capt. Douglass Ottinger took command of *Lawrence*.

On November 18, 1851, the brig sailed from San Francisco for Monterey, where it arrived on November 20, picked up Collector William Russell, and cleared for San Francisco. After a brief stop at Santa Cruz, *Lawrence* anchored off Point Lobos on the evening of November 25. The tide had ebbed and ran with a strong set to the south, bucking the incoming swell from the west. After an hour of rough seas sweeping the decks, *Lawrence's* anchor cable parted. Driving south, the brig struck the beach about four miles south of Point Lobos at 9:00 p.m.

> *The vessel first struck in 3 1/2 fathoms water, and in the next breaker came down with such tremendous force, that it appeared as if every seam and timber in her must have started. At the same time, tons of water fell on our decks. By changing the position of the sails, the ship's head was kept toward the beach and stern to the breakers. . . . The vessel then laid bows toward the land, continuing to strike very heavily, and force her way through heavy combing seas toward the beach.*

The next morning the crew took a hawser and hove *Lawrence* up on the beach. For the next three days they labored to strip the wreck of "papers, navigation instruments, small arms, ammunition," cannon, sails, rigging, yards, chains, hawsers, and provisions.

Lawrence was not salvaged despite Capt. Ottinger's belief that the brig could be got off; "but the expense attending it with the requisite repairs would doubtless amount to a much larger sum than will replace her with a more suitable vessel for Revenue duty on this coast. The sailing qualities of the "Lawrence" were very ordinary. . . ." A small schooner, *Frolic*, was chartered to replace *Lawrence*. Outfitted with the brig's guns and gear and manned by its crew, *Frolic* had an interesting career in the Revenue service that included assistance to a number of vessels wrecked near the Golden Gate. The wrecked

hulk of *Lawrence* was sold at auction in January 1852. The wreck remained visible for some time and was marked on a survey of Ocean Beach done in mid-1852. No further mention was made.

Julia Castner
June 28, 1859

The bark *Julia Castner* was built at East Milford, Delaware in 1858 for William and John Somers, Samuel and John Castner of Philadelphia, and Alexander McNeill of New Orleans. Registered at Philadelphia, the 509-ton bark was sent around the Horn into the Pacific on its maiden voyage. On June 28, 1859, having recently arrived at San Francisco from Puget Sound, *Julia Castner* was hauling from Vallejo Street Wharf to Steuart Street Wharf to complete ballasting when it capsized off Clay Street Wharf. The vessel began to drift. The steamer *San Antonio* caught *Julia Castner* and moored it to the clipper ship *Southern Eagle*. During the evening of June 29, *Julia Castner* went adrift in a seven-knot current and was swept out the Golden Gate, wrecking on Ocean Beach. By the next day the bark was a total loss:

> *She is laying about a mile to the southard of Point Lobos, on the beach, about a quarter of a mile out from high water mark, with the rollers washing over her. Efforts have been made to save some of her spars, but to no purpose, as the seas are too heavy for any small boat to live, and with the exception of what may be washed high and dry, nothing will be saved.*

The stranded hulk of the Italian bark Brignardello *disintegrates in the surf near the Cliff House during the winter of 1868.*

The remains of the vessel were not formally salvaged. Oral tradition in San Francisco insists that timbers from a shipwrecked vessel, possibly *Julia Castner*, near Point Lobos were used to build the Seal Rock House on Ocean Beach around 1859.

F.W. Bailey
January 8, 1863

The 711-ton ship *F.W. Bailey* was built at Freeport, Maine in 1854 for C. Cushing & Co., who owned the ship throughout its career. *Bailey* was apparently engaged in the general carrying trade, and arrived at San Francisco on November 30, 1862 from Bordeaux, France. Clearing San Francisco the following January 8 in ballast for Puget Sound to load lumber for Australia, *Bailey* was lost after leaving harbor. Still under the command of the pilot, Capt. Callot, *F.W. Bailey* began to drift toward shore off the South Head (Point Lobos). "It was found utterly impossible to wear her off . . . the anchor was let go. The chain, however. . . . cut her bow down to the water's edge, and the craft drifted ashore."

The ship struck the beach three miles south of Point Lobos. "There was no wind, but a very heavy sea." A lowered boat was swamped. A second boat was then lowered, and the second mate, the carpenter, and three seamen leapt in and drifted to the beach. They went for help as the ship began to break up in the surf. Of the seventeen people on board when *F.W. Bailey* wrecked, only eight were saved, including the pilot. Among the dead were Capt. Lemuel P. Dyer, the mate, the cabin boy, the cook, and six seamen. The wreck of *F.W. Bailey* was the first with great loss of life on Ocean Beach. The body of the captain washed ashore along with the mate and cabin boy. No others were recovered. The following day visitors to the beach reported that *F.W. Bailey* was "fast going to pieces. As she breaks up, the detached pieces come ashore. The beach is strewn with fragments. Judging from the heavy surf beating upon the ill-fated ship, it cannot be long before she completely disappears."

Beeswing
February 1863

The schooner *Beeswing* was owned and operated by San Francisco mariners and merchants Robert Young and Thomas McRea and carried a variety of merchandise between Monterey and San Francisco. On its last voyage in February 1863, for example, it arrived at San Francisco thirty-eight hours out of Monterey with 100 barrels of oil, 40 steer hides, 120 trees, 4 boxes of cheese, and 5 boxes of merchandise. Loading a return cargo for Monterey, *Beeswing* cleared San Francisco a few days later for Monterey but encountered gale-force winds off the San Francisco Bar. The bark *Ork* from Humboldt reported seeing an unidentified schooner founder on the bar and that *Ork* had sailed through flotsam that included cans of oil and camphene and boxes of candles. News of a wreck off Point San Pedro with survivors clinging to the hull in the heavy surf resulted in the dispatch of the tug *Monitor*. Steaming eight miles south of Point Lobos, *Monitor*'s crew saw the wreck of *Beeswing* ashore near

Mussel Rock, broken and wedged into the rocks, "her pumps being forced up, her masts and bulwarks gone, and her ribs sticking out from the deck." All eleven persons on board perished, including two owners and four passengers from Monterey.

Ann Parry
January 4, 1865

Built at Portsmouth, New Hampshire, on the banks of the Piscataqua River in 1825 for two local merchants, the ship *Ann Parry* enjoyed a long career, first as a "tramp" carrying assorted cargoes for hire, then as a whaler. Sailing from Portsmouth in 1832, *Ann Parry* made several voyages into the Pacific until 1849. Then, like many other old vessels, the ship was swept up into the California gold rush. Re-registered at Salem, Massachusetts in June 1849, *Ann Parry*, now rerigged as a bark, sailed for San Francisco with four passengers under the command of Capt. W.M. Harron on June 21, 1849. One of the last vessels to arrive at San Francisco in 1849, the bark sailed through the Golden Gate on December 29, 184 days out. *Ann Parry* was a workhorse in the burgeoning coastal trade. Sold in 1850, the bark became an early participant in the Pacific Coast lumber trade, and arrived at San Francisco on November 30, 1850 with 276,000 board feet of lumber from Port Madison, Washington. The bark's coasting career was interrupted in 1858 when *Ann Parry* carried one hundred passengers to the recently discovered gold fields on British Columbia's Fraser River. *Ann Parry* returned to San Francisco on September 11, 1858 and once again entered the lumber trade, regularly sailing between Puget Sound and San Francisco and surviving a stranding in Washington in 1860.

On January 3, 1865, *Ann Parry* arrived off the Golden Gate laden with three hundred thousand board feet of lumber and 250 sacks of Washington potatoes. The ship anchored outside the Gate "owing to the fog and want of a fair breeze . . . and lay off the bar for the night." During the evening the seas became rough, and *Ann Parry* dragged in to the beach, grounding a "few hundred yards" south of the Cliff House the next morning.

The wreck broke up in the surf, drowning Capt. Trask and three of his crew. A week later a newspaper account read:

> *It lies high and dry on the beach. . . . The hull seems to have broken entirely up, and the stout masts were snapped in pieces, and her timbers torn and splintered. . . . The bulk of the lumber lies in a single pile, upon the wreck of the hull, fragments of the masts, the capstan, and other heavy articles, lying on top of all. A portion of the lumber, and large pieces of the deck and sides of the vessel, were carried by the waves further in shore and scattered on the beach. . . .*

Local residents scavenged what they could from the wreck. A gang of Chinese laborers hired by *Ann Parry*'s owner, Capt. Chase of San Francisco, saved what they could of the cargo and timbers. The sacks of potatoes, buried beneath the lumber, were sold for $60 to Capt. Junius Foster, proprietor of the Cliff House.

Brignardello

September 3, 1868

The 543-ton bark *Brignardello* was built in Genoa, Italy in 1865 for Stefano Brignardello and Giovanni Battista Machiavello, "manufacturers, macaroni and vermicelli, ship bread, etc.," of San Francisco and Genoa, Italy. The bark made only two voyages to San Francisco, and wrecked on the second one. On September 3, 1868, *Brignardello*, under the command of Capt. Mazzini, lay off the Golden Gate after a fifty-four-day passage from Valparaiso, Chile. The captain, pilotless and unable to take bearings in the thick fog, attempted to make the Gate when he saw breakers ahead.

Instantly the helmsman brought the vessel "hard aport," not knowing which way the beach trended, but hoping to head off shore. Not being able to see land, all was guesswork. The bark ended squarely on the beach. *Brignardello* grounded in the surf on the beach directly south of Point Lobos, just under the Cliff House in "Kelly's Cove." The crew managed to reach shore in boats, and when the tide fell, landed what goods they could from the wreck, "some of the men standing in the surf up to their middle while handling casks, bundles, etc."

Brignardello lay perpendicular to the shore, bow

The ship (later a bark) King Philip (L) was wrecked on Ocean Beach on January 25, 1878. This is the only known photograph of the ship. King Philip was in Australia for repairs on a transpacific voyage.

to the beach and stern covered at low tide by eight feet of water. The wreck lay in a spectacular location, and thousands of San Franciscans flocked to the beach. Salvage proceeded slowly: by September 5, only sailors' dunnage and a few spars had been sent ashore. The effort increased over the next few days. Laborers built staging from shore to the wreck, and one thousand cases of nuts were landed, but surf collapsed the staging. Surf pounding against the stern opened *Brignardello*'s seams, and by early September, six feet of water lay in the hold.

Attempts to pull the bark free failed. On September 12, 1868, it was sold with cargo "as she now lies." The cargo was lucrative: 200 tons of marble slabs, 2,500 boxes of olive oil, 3,000 bags of almonds, 30 boxes of cheese, 60 bales of paper, 100 sacks of wheat, 200 sacks of chicory, 400 boxes of Bath Brick, 50 cases of Vermouth, and 4 cases of Blacking. L.R. Meyer of San Francisco purchased the wreck for $8,050; "the marble alone — if it can be got out — is worth more than that sum, and the purchaser has a chance of making a good thing." Meyer dispatched the steam tug *Goliah* to land a barge and pump for salvage assistance. Work progressed well: "the greater portion of the cargo . . . has already been beached in safety."

The salvage operations continued through September. As the cargo was removed, *Brignardello* began to list to starboard. Meyer abandoned his efforts in October, having regained his investment. The wreck of *Brignardello*, along with about seventy tons of marble, thirty tons of sulphur, twenty tons of "miscellaneous merchandise," and two quarter-boats left on board was offered for sale again. On October 10, 1868, the vessel was purchased at auction by San Francisco shipbuilder J.C. Cousins, who paid $700 for the hulk. "From the price realized, one would conclude that the chances of getting her afloat were slight. There is still some marble in her hold, though the bulk of the cargo has been discharged."

Brignardello remained in the surf through the winter of 1868. Unable to do much with the hulk, Cousins sold it. Late December storms tore at the exposed wreck, and "the heavy seas breaking completely over her, swept away the cabin, galley, and forward house . . . and turned her over on her port side." Finally, in early 1869, as winter storms battered the hulk, the new owner, a Mr. Bruce, began to break the ship up:

> *All hope of saving her has been abandoned; and men were at work yesterday cutting away everything they could get at, and hauling it ashore. The foremast, which had stood intact through all the vessel's disasters, was cut away . . . and fell with a tremendous crash into the ocean, carrying with it everything above the deck save the short stump of the hindmast. It was secured by a line attached to a windlass on the beach, by which it was hauled ashore.*

In order to salvage as much of the vessel's copper fastenings and timbers, Bruce planned to blow up *Brignardello* with black powder and "gather up the fragments, that nothing more may be lost. The explosion . . . will tear into fragments what was but a short time since as staunch and fine a vessel of her class as ever rode the waves. . . . " The local press made no further mention of the wrecked *Brignardello*.

Aimer

June 26, 1871

The two-masted schooner *Aimer*, built at Coos Bay, Oregon in 1870, was a small coasting vessel registered at 96.25 tons. *Aimer* joined a large number of small two-masted schooners in the Pacific Coast lumber trade, carrying lumber and occasionally general cargo from small logging ports to San Francisco. On Monday, June 26, 1871, the schooner arrived off San Francisco with 140 tons of coal, thirty-five thousand board feet of lumber, and some cord wood from Coos Bay.

Dense fog and a strong southerly current caused *Aimer*'s master to miss his bearings while the schooner drifted past the Golden Gate. A light from the Ocean-Side House (a structure located at what is now the intersection of Vicente Street and the Great Highway) was mistaken for the light at Point Bonita, the northern head of the harbor entrance. As the captain tacked for what he thought was the Golden Gate, *Aimer* sailed into the breakers. The crew

The whaling bark Atlantic's *crushed and scattered remains on Ocean Beach, 1886. Thirty-two men were "beaten and bruised" by the wreckage and held underwater. Their deaths made this the worse shipwreck on Ocean Beach.*

dropped the anchors, but they failed to hold, and *Aimer* soon went up on the beach and filled with water. The vessel landed "on the beach abreast of the Ocean-Side House."

The chances of getting *Aimer* off were slight. The cargo was lost, and though "the rigging and sails will probably be saved . . . the vessel will go to pieces, as as the sea is making a great breach in her." The damage was substantial as beachcombers joined the surf in stripping the schooner of mainmast, bowsprit, two deck beams, and part of the mainrail and bulwarks. Amazingly, the wreck held together sufficiently to be pulled free of the beach on August 9, 1871. However, on the final tow, the hawsers attached to the water-logged hulk parted, and *Aimer* once again went ashore broadside and was abandoned.

Eliza

January 31, 1871

The ten-ton sloop *Eliza* was built at San Pedro, California in 1868 for the fishing trade. Owned by "three Greek fishermen," *Eliza* left Meiggs' wharf, San Francisco on January 31, 1871 for Sonoma with one thousand pounds of fish. One of her owners, the sloop's captain (unnamed in the wreck accounts), was the only person on board. He sailed across the bay but lost the wind near Sausalito. Attempting to anchor, he found "he had not cable enough . . . bent the main sheet on . . . went below, where he turned in and went to sleep." Caught by the outgoing tide, *Eliza* drifted out past the Golden Gate. At 1:00 p.m. *Eliza* went ashore on the rocks at Point Lobos. The captain rushed to the

deck and was washed overboard by the surf. He caught hold of the stern gearing, but was torn free, and "floundered around in the water" until thrown up onto a rock near shore. A neighboring rancher waded into the rough surf and pulled the him ashore. *Eliza* was a total loss.

Josephine Wilcutt

January 24, 1872

The eighty-six-ton, two-masted schooner *Josephine Wilcutt*, built at San Francisco in 1860, was engaged in the Pacific Coast lumber trade and was owned by the Mendocino Lumber Company. *Josephine Wilcutt* wrecked at Mendocino in early April 1867 when heavy seas caused her and the schooner *Mendocino* to part moorings and go ashore. Despite the opinion of the San Francisco *Daily Alta California* that *Josephine Wilcutt* "will probably be totally lost," the schooner was gotten off. On January 24, 1872, *Josephine Wilcutt* was again wrecked, blown ashore at Point Lobos while departing San Francisco. Loaded with provisions for "a mill in Mendocino county," the schooner was tossed on to the rocks north of the Cliff House. "The rocks forced a hole through her bottom, and the waves making a complete breach over her decks soon rendered her a complete wreck. She is now in pieces, and the adjacent beach is strewn with portions of the vessel and cargo."

The wreck of *Josephine Wilcutt* was followed two months later by the loss of another Mendocino Lumber Company vessel, the schooner *Ella Florence*, which wrecked on the Mendocino Coast in March

1872. The *West Coast Signal* noted that the firm "has been particularly unfortunate," losing the schooner *Brilliant*, *Josephine Wilcutt*, and *Ella Florence* in the space of a year, "wiping out their stock of coasting vessels."

King Philip
January 25, 1878

The 1194-ton, three-masted ship (later a bark) *King Philip* was constructed by Dennett Weymouth at Alna, Maine in 1856. Built for William T. Glidden of Boston, the ship was engaged in the general carrying trade, sailing from Boston to ports in Europe, South America, and the Pacific. In March 1869 one or more mutinous crew members set the ship on fire at Honolulu. *King Philip*'s bow and forecastle were seriously damaged, and it was condemned and sold at auction. The ship was purchased by Pope and Talbot of San Francisco, lumber merchants, who repaired it at their Port Gamble, Washington, lumber yard.

Operating under the Pope and Talbot flag, *King Philip* continued in general trade, principally shipping guano and grain to Europe. In May 1874 another mutinous crew set the ship on fire off Annapolis, Maryland. Once the fire was extinguished and the crew subdued, *King Philip* continued on. The fire had damaged the hull, though, and the ship put in at Rio de Janeiro for repairs. After a long delay *King Philip* finally reached San Francisco in May 1875, but Pope and Talbot never sent it around Cape Horn again. In September 1876 it was re-rigged as a bark, with a reduced rig to better sail coastwise in the Pacific Coast

lumber trade. In 1878 it was reported that *"King Philip* has just completed her tenth trip to Puget Sound and back since January 1st 1876, and has still some days to spare. She has brought to port in that time nearly ten million feet in lumber."

On January 25, 1878, *King Philip* departed San Francisco harbor in ballast for Port Gamble, Washington. Off the San Francisco Bar the wind fell. The assisting tug left to rescue the distressed ship *Western Shore*. *King Philip*, anchors failing to hold, dragged ashore on Ocean Beach at 5:00 p.m. Wind drove the ship high up on the beach at high tide. At low tide the bark was high and dry, and sightseers were able to walk up to and touch the hull. The vessel remained intact. "Yesterday morning at and after daylight the sea was breaking well up to the vessel, and she moved very uneasily at times, but later in the day it appeared as if she had settled down in the sand . . . she was immovable."

Surf washing around the hull caused *King Philip* to sink deeper into the sand until sixteen feet of the hull lay buried. On January 26, 1878, the stranded hulk sold at auction for $1,050 to John Molloy of San Francisco. Molloy stripped *King Philip*, cut away the masts, and blasted the upper hull apart with black powder to salvage metal fastenings and timber. Lower portions of the vessel remained buried on the beach, visible though the end of the nineteenth century. In January 1886 when the whaling bark *Atlantic* went ashore near *King Philip*, accounts mentioned that the frames of the latter wreck still showed. In 1902 when the three-masted schooner *Reporter* was lost at the same site, newspaper accounts noted that the "bones" of *King Philip* could be seen. The flattening of the

The two-masted schooner Neptune, *stranded on Ocean Beach on the afternoon of August 10, 1900.*

beach dune field in the early decades of the twentieth century to build the Great Highway buried *King Philip*'s remains.

W.H. Gawley
October 23, 1880

The 483-ton barkentine *W.H. Gawley* was built in 1861 at Port Townsend, Washington from the burnt-out hulk of the ship *Northern Eagle.* Engaged in the lumber trade, *W.H. Gawley* was carrying four hundred thousand board feet of lumber from Port Madison, Washington when it was lost attempting to enter San Francisco harbor on the foggy morning of October 23, 1880. The vessel ran aground on Ocean Beach about five miles south of Fulton Street when the captain lost his bearings. Lying three hundred yards from the beach on an even keel in quiet water, *W.H. Gawley* remained tight. Taking a boat to shore, the second mate and four seamen walked to the Cliff House to seek help.

The tug *Rescue* was dispatched from San Francisco and arrived at the wreck by mid-morning. Three female passengers were taken aboard the tug, and the effort to save *W.H. Gawley* began:

> *Men were busy tossing her deck-load of lumber overboard, and the tug . . . was snorting and straining in a vigorous effort to haul her off into deep water. Her topsails were set, her remaining sails were clewed and furled, her port-anchor was down, and such other*

> *dispositions had been made as might aid the endeavor to pull her afloat. . . .*

The effort failed when the barkentine would not move. The hull had given way and *W.H. Gawley* was full of water. The following day the surf came up, knocking *W.H. Gawley* on the port side. The crew from the Golden Gate Life-Saving Service had been standing by, and fired a line to the vessel with a Lyle gun. With the help of several hundred spectators, the crew and captain of *W.H. Gawley* were hauled ashore on the breeches buoy. On October 27 the wreck began to break up, and by the twentieth "she had gone to pieces, the lumber with which she was laden being scattered far and along the beach."

Dublin
August 31, 1882

The 706-ton bark *Dublin* was built at Brunswick, Maine, in 1839. By 1879 the vessel was registered at San Francisco and engaged in the Pacific Coast lumber trade. On August 31, 1882, *Dublin*, under the command of Capt. Maloney, was off the Heads with a cargo of lumber from Seabeck, Washington. The thick fog lifted enough for the captain to take his bearings, and as the fog again covered the water he ordered the course changed to make the Golden Gate. Losing his reckoning, Maloney sailed the bark ashore.

Dublin struck Ocean Beach two miles south of the Cliff House at 6 p.m. The timbers parted and the bark flooded until it lay on the bottom in twelve feet of

The Neptune's broken hull was found in 1982 on the beach of Fort Funston, nestled against the cliffs at nearly the same location the schooner was lost in 1900.

water. The crew lowered a boat and some went ashore for help. After being notified, the tugs *Katie, Holyoke, Donald,* and *Etna* steamed to Ocean Beach to pull the wrecked bark free. On the first attempt the hawser parted, and on the second the bitts tore free. "Her captain and crew, with their personal effects, went on board the tugs and came in, leaving the *Dublin,* with her head on and sails clewed, to her fate.

Atlantic
December 16, 1886

The 366-ton bark *Atlantic* was built at New Bedford, Mass. in 1851 for the whaling trade. *Atlantic* sailed from New Bedford on October 31, 1851 for the Atlantic whaling grounds and was gone for three years, returning with 1,097 barrels of sperm whale oil, 196 barrels of whale oil, and 600 lbs. of whalebone. *Atlantic* sailed from New Bedford on October 14, 1854 for the Pacific Ocean whaling grounds, returning five years later, on May 28, 1859, with 1,170 barrels of sperm-oil. On May 1, 1860, the ship again cleared for the Pacific, returning four years later with 211 barrels of sperm oil and 10 barrels of whale-oil.

Sold to whaling fleet magnates William R. and Joseph Wing, *Atlantic* did not sail again until the Civil War ended. Since large numbers of American merchant vessels were being swept from the seas by Confederate raiders and a number of whalers had been burnt in the North Pacific by the Confederate raider *Shenandoah, Atlantic*'s eighteen-month lay-up was a wise decision. The bark made five extended whaling voyages from New Bedford between 1865 and 1881. Beginning in 1881, *Atlantic* began to sail out of San Francisco, by then the principal whaling port in the United States with the decline of the Atlantic whale fishery and the rise of the North Pacific and Arctic fisheries. For the next five years the whaler made short voyages of less than a year's duration.

Arriving at San Francisco on November 16, 1886, with six hundred barrels of oil and eleven thousand pounds of whalebone, *Atlantic* was readied for the next year in the Arctic. A month later, on December 16, the bark cleared San Francisco for the last time. Towed by tug out the Golden Gate, *Atlantic* anchored off the bar when the wind died. Caught in a heavy swell, the ship began to drift toward shore. Capt. Warren weighed anchor and tried to work *Atlantic* off. When that failed, the crew dropped anchor, to no avail. *Atlantic* went ashore on Ocean Beach about one thousand yards south of the exposed remains of *King Philip*.

Atlantic's hull was in poor condition and it quickly disintegrated in the surf. Waves tore off the bow, drowning many of the sailors asleep in the forecastle. The hull was crushed, casting the remainder of the crew into the surf. Entangled in loose rigging and surrounded by floating debris, many crew members were "beaten and bruised" and held under the surface. Of the forty-three men on board, only eleven survived, including Capt. Warren. The wreck of the *Atlantic* was the worst maritime disaster on Ocean Beach.

News of the wreck attracted a crowd of fifty thousand who flocked to the beach and collected souvenirs; "nothing that was portable escaped the collectors—ropes, pieces of sail, pulleys, handspikes and tackle of all descriptions were carried away." Because of the high loss of life and allegations that the ship was unseaworthy, the U.S. Life-Saving Service held an investigation and found that *Atlantic* was unsound, that Capt. Warren had not exercised proper judgement in casting off from his tug inside the bar and for not alerting the sleeping men in the forecastle. *Atlantic*'s owner, William R. Wing, and Capt. Warren were censured and indicted for manslaughter in the deaths of the seamen. The captain skipped town, and after initial indignation the case quieted down. *Atlantic*'s battered remains, spread out over a mile on the beach, quickly disappeared beneath surf and sand, leaving no trace of the "Atlantic Horror."

Parallel
January 15, 1887

The 148-ton, two-masted schooner *Parallel* was built in 1868 at San Francisco. Owned by S.E. Peterson of San Francisco, *Parallel* was one of hundreds of "work-a-day" craft plying the coast. Clearing the Golden Gate on January 13, 1887 for Astoria, Oregon, with a typically varied cargo of hay, pig iron, kerosene, oak planks, and forty-two tons of black powder, *Parallel* was unable to beat against the head winds and make the open sea. The tide, setting to the south, also blocked progress. *Parallel* struggled for westing for two days off Point Lobos before Capt. Miller finally gave up the fight. As the schooner was about to go on the rocks at Point Lobos, the captain gave the order to abandon ship. The nine-man crew pulled away from *Parallel* as fast as they could, "fearing she would strike at any moment,

A crowd gathers near the toppled mizzenmast of the three-masted schooner Reporter, *1902.*

and knowing the dangerous contents. . . ."

Parallel grounded south of Point Lobos "into the little bay to the south of the Cliff House, which is being remodeled by Adolph Sutro into an aquarium [Sutro Baths]" at 9:30 p.m. on January 15. A crew from the United States Life-Saving Station at Golden Gate Park responded to the wreck. Finding no one on board, the life-savers posted watchmen and retired for the evening. At 12:34 a.m. on January 16, the powder in *Parallel*'s hold was detonated by the schooner's jarring against the rocks. The explosion obliterated the schooner, demolished much of the Cliff House, threw debris over a mile in every direction, and woke most of San Francisco. The watchmen were thrown over a hundred yards, and were seriously injured but survived.

Parallel's crew, meanwhile, had rowed into the Golden Gate, landed at Sausalito, and after being transported to San Fransisco, rode out to the beach to see what was left of their schooner. They were not alone; more than fifty thousand San Franciscans flocked to the scene:

To the general astonishment, not a vestige of the wreck remained. Not so much as a floating barrel, bit of spar, or splinter of rail lay along the beach. Every bit of flotsam and jetsam had been carried off by the relic-hunters, and even the sand-dunes several hundred yards away were minutely searched in hope of finding a shred of sail or rigging or sliver of wood that belonged to the "Parallel." "Fakirs" materially assisted the relic hunters, and accommodatingly sold them at fancy prices bits of rope yarn, sections of ratlines and shrouds and squares of weatherbeaten sailcloth procured at city junkshops.

Capt. Miller was sharply criticized for abandoning his vessel and for not alerting the lifesavers or area residents of the schooner's dangerous cargo when he arrived at Sausalito. Investigation disclosed that he had not even anchored *Parallel* to try and keep off the rocks, fearing the jarring of the chain would set the powder off.

William Frederick
July 3, 1887

The forty–two-ton, two-masted schooner *William Frederick* was built at San Francisco in 1863 for the lumber trade. On July 2, 1887, *William Frederick*, with a four-man crew consisting of Capt. Martin Johnson and seamen Fred Jacobsen, William Keyser, and Jacob Demick, sailed from San Francisco for Russian Landing to load lumber. Off the San Francisco Bar, however, *William Frederick* was becalmed and began to drift ashore with the current. Capt. Johnson attempted to sail against the current but could make no headway.

The following day *William Frederick* struck on the beach below Sloat Boulevard. Both anchors were dropped, and this prevented *William Frederick* from going ashore. The schooner *Anna Matilda* discovered *William Frederick* and took off the crew. Later the captain and two of the men "returned to the schooner to get their clothes. Finding that it was impossible to board . . . the men, despite the advice of Captain Johnson, determined to go ashore through the breakers. The boat was capsized and the two men drowned." Capt. Johnson struggled ashore and made his way to the United States Life-Saving Station at the foot of Sloat Boulevard. Rescuers searched unsuccessfully for the bodies of the drowned sailors (Jacobsen and Keyser). The tug *Rescue* was dispatched to pull *William Frederick* free. "It was impossible, however, to reach the craft, and when the tide ebbed she was left high and dry on the beach with her bottom knocked out, a total wreck."

The wreck was looted by local residents despite the best efforts of the Life-Saving Service. The "sails, rigging, anchors, pumps, etc." were saved, and sold at auction for $370. The wrecked hulk of *William Frederick* brought only $5, sold to John Molloy, a San Francisco grocer who salvaged wrecks.

Bessie Everding
September 9, 1888

The seventy-three-ton, two-masted schooner *Bessie Everding* was built at San Francisco in 1876. *Bessie Everding* was one of more than five hundred two-masters operating on the Pacific Coast in the last decades of the nineteenth century, carrying a variety of cargoes between ports. *Bessie Everding* was built for the Pacific Coast lumber trade, and at the time of loss was bound for San Francisco from Bowen's Landing, California with a cargo of firewood and railroad ties valued at $1,600.

Anchoring off the San Francisco Bar on the evening of September 9, 1888, Capt. Jorgensen and his five-man crew were unaware of *Bessie Everding*'s slow drift toward the beach as thick fog obscured the land. "Soon the seas broke over her, and the crew . . . not knowing their position, took to their boat and safely reached San Francisco. . . ." A patrolling surfman from the Golden Gate Park Station of the United States Life-Saving Service noticed firewood and railroad ties washing up on the beach, and as he walked south of the station, he heard a cat's meow to seaward. Flashing his lamp, he saw the dim outline of a vessel in the breakers and ran for help. When the Life-Saving Station surfboat reached the wreck, however, they found *Bessie Everding* abandoned by all save the ship's cat.

When the tide fell the life-savers were able to board the schooner and note her condition. A message was sent to San Francisco, and in the morning Capt. Jorgensen and the cook arrived on the scene. *Bessie Everding*, lying about a mile south of the station at the foot of Lawton Street on Ocean Beach, was stripped of sails, rigging, and useful fittings. Half the cargo was salvaged, and *Bessie Everding* was abandoned to break up in the surf.

William L. Beebe
December 10, 1894

The 281-ton three-masted schooner *William L. Beebe* was built at Seattle, Washington in 1875. *William L. Beebe* was engaged for its entire career in the Pacific Coast lumber trade, and when wrecked was bringing a cargo of lumber from Port Blakely, Washington to San Francisco. After a rough eleven-day passage, *William L. Beebe* arrived off the San Francisco Bar at 5:30 a.m. on December 10, 1894. The sea was smooth, and the schooner was crossing the bar when:

> *Suddenly and without warning an immense breaker rolled over the stern . . . carrying away the wheelhouse and knocking Olsen [the crewman at the wheel] from his position. . . . the first wave practically staggered the* Beebe. *She did not respond readily to the helm and became unmanageable.*

The rudder and mizzen-mast rigging had also been swept away. There was no wind, and the vessel broadsided as it drifted south along the edge of the bar, with occasional breakers boarding it.

Finally, at 7:30 a.m., *William L. Beebe* grounded on Ocean Beach near the foot of Sloat Boulevard. "She

The four-masted bark Gifford *regularly sailed between Australia and California.*

Only the foremast and the stub of the jiggermast remain standing as Gifford is pounded by the sea in October 1902.

dove into the sand in a most remarkable manner, becoming imbedded so firmly that there was no possibility of her getting off." The crew took to the rigging as the heavy surf swept the decks. Crews from the United States Life-Saving Service stations on Ocean Beach responded to the wreck. The surf, full of loose lumber from *Beebe's* cargo, was too rough to launch a lifeboat from the beach. A Lyle gun was set up and a line was fired to the schooner, but the line landed on the deck and could not be reached. The next three attempts also failed as the line was tangled in debris; on the fifth try, however, the line was secured and the crew was safely brought to the shore by breeches buoy.

    William L. Beebe had wrecked at high tide. As the tide receded, the schooner sat high and dry on the beach. "She has a big hole in her bow and is buried up to her water-line in sand, which makes it impossible to float her. Within a week or two she will probably have sunk nearly out of sight. About the only use that can be made of her is for firewood. . . ." The schooner was a total loss, and sold to Capt. A.C. Freese of San Francisco for $255. "The Captain considered that he had made a very good purchase for the winches and anchors will bring more than that. He is of the opinion that he can wreck the vessel from the beach. The masts and booms will be saved intact, and the rigging, with the exception of the mizzen shrouds, is all right." The salvors stripped *William L. Beebe* of useable fittings before the hulk was battered to pieces and disappeared beneath surf and sand.

Neptune
August 10, 1900

The 184-ton, two-masted schooner *Neptune* was built by Hans D. Bendixsen at Fairhaven, California in 1882. Built for the lumber trade at a time when three-masted schooners were beginning to take over, *Neptune* was by economic necessity a large two-master, 106.5 feet long. *Neptune* was owned by a variety of owners, but at the time of loss, the controlling owner was Robert Dollar of San Francisco. Dollar, a former lumber mill operator, had begun his own shipping company in 1888. Business was booming by 1900, and by 1930 Dollar Lines was one of the biggest shipping firms in the United States.

    Neptune's career consisted of dozens of short voyages along the coast each year, carrying milled lumber, pilings, and railroad ties from small coast mills to market in San Francisco. When the schooner departed from San Francisco on July 25, 1900, it was chartered by the lumber firm of Sudden and Christensen to load shingles and pilings at the Northern California port of Houda Landing and bring them back to San Francisco. Sailing in ballast on the twenty-fifth, *Neptune* was back in port August 4, having discovered a leak.

    Neptune, dry docked and repaired, was ready to sail on August 10, 1900. On that date, according to Capt. Johnson,

> *We sailed from Main-street wharf. . . . at 1 o'clock and became becalmed after getting outside the Heads. We began drifting toward Mussel Rock, and as we approached the shore*

we became caught in a strong and dangerous current that sets inshore at that point. We dropped both the schooner's anchors, but they failed to hold. Then we launched the boats and put out what is known as a cat anchor. The schooner kept drifting in spite of all we could do to prevent it and we were soon on the sand.

Neptune was stranded on the beach two miles south of the United States Life-Saving Service station at Sloat Boulevard, six miles south of Point Lobos. The life-savers saw *Neptune* go ashore and quickly responded with their beach cart to rescue Capt. Johnson and his crew. *Neptune*, aground with seams open, was pounding on the hard sand. Late that evening the tug *Alert* was dispatched, but by the time *Alert* steamed out past the Golden Gate, the tide had fallen and *Neptune* was high and dry on the beach.

By the morning of August 11 *Neptune* had been pushed even higher up on the beach. "The little vessel is in a worse position than if she had struck on the rocks, for the reason that she is imbedded in the quicksand, and the wash of the waves will soon throw up a barrier around her that will be hard to dig away." The editors of the San Francisco *Examiner* noted that "it is the opinion of nautical men that she will remain where she is until a storm breaks her up and scatters her bones along the beach." On August 12, 1900, the

The steam schooner Aberdeen was torn apart on the bar and washed ashore on Ocean Beach in January 1916.

San Francisco *Chronicle* reported *Neptune* as a "total loss." One last attempt to pull the schooner free on August 12 failed; the two tugs involved, unable to budge *Neptune*, departed that afternoon, "leaving the ill-fated vessel to bleach its bones on the beach."

Eureka
June 19, 1902

The 295-ton, three-masted barkentine *Eureka* was built by Charles Murray at Indian Island on Humboldt Bay, California. Launched on October 31, 1868, *Eureka* was 134.3 feet long. Just prior to launch, the local paper described *Eureka* as "a model in which are skillfully combined the four great essentials: beauty, strength, speed and capacity. . . . our town may feel justly proud that her name is borne by such a staunch and beautiful craft. . . ." *Eureka* was built to carry lumber and passengers from Humboldt Bay sawmills to San Francisco and bring back general cargo. The maiden voyage was auspicious; *Eureka* sailed from *Eureka* to San Francisco in thirty hours, and then returned in twenty-four hours.

Eureka had a long, successful career. Around 1900 the yards were sent down from the foremast and the barkentine was re-rigged as a three-masted schooner. Departing Meiggs' wharf, San Francisco, on June 19, 1902, *Eureka* cleared for Eureka to load lumber for the owners, the Charles Nelson Company. Sailing through thick fog, Capt. Shou did not realize that the current had caught his vessel and pulled it south of the Heads. At 9 o'clock that evening, Shou, believing

Aberdeen's intact transom, part of a mile-wide scatter of wreckage on the beach after the steamer's wreck.

he was four miles offshore, ordered *Eureka* on a port tack. "The peak was lowered and the topsail clewed up, and, all of a sudden, the first thing we knew, she struck bow on." *Eureka* had gone aground on the beach near Mussel Rock, five miles southeast of the foot of Sloat Boulevard.

Surf swept the decks. Shou ordered the crew and his wife, who regularly sailed with him (as did many wives of Pacific Coast lumber skippers), into the ship's boat. The boat was swamped, but they managed to right it and struggle through the surf to shore, where they built a driftwood fire to dry themselves. The crew at the United States Life-Saving Service station at Sloat Boulevard learned of the wreck at 10:30 and responded. They found some of the crew ashore, the others in the boat attempting to salvage what they could from *Eureka*, by then lying broadside to the breakers, the bow pointed toward Mussel Rock. The station launched a surfboat, and the life-savers helped remove what they could from *Eureka*, including compasses and chronometer. "When nothing further could be done, the crew returned to station."

Morning "disclosed that there was no hope for her. Her worn-out timbers and frame had given in to the battering of the surf and sand, and her hold was rapidly filling with water, the garboard strakes having parted company with the keel." Capt. Shou and his crew remained at the wreck, camping next to the cliffs in a small niche that they filled with items salvaged from *Eureka*:

> *The personal property of the schooner's crew made a strange assortment. There were big, white canvas bags—one for each man—two weather-beaten old trunks, two old hampers, several baskets and more boxes, and a red plush-covered whirling chair, another old red plush armchair, a rocking chair, and old-fashioned marble-top table that had been the elaborate sitting room furniture of the captain's cabin.*

On June 20 a wagon dispatched from the Life-Saving Station carried away the salvaged items and crew. Shou remained to guard the ship, but it was a total loss. On June 24 *Eureka*'s battered bones were sold to Harry Goodall of San Francisco for $105.

Reporter
March 13, 1902

The 351-ton, three-masted schooner *Reporter* was built at Port Ludlow, Washington by the Hall Brothers, noted Pacific Coast shipbuilders, in 1876. *Reporter* spent its years sailing in the Pacific Coast lumber trade, bringing milled lumber, shingles, and pilings from small coastal logging ports to San Francisco. When lost, *Reporter*'s managing owner was the E.K. Wood Lumber Company of San Francisco. After loading a cargo of four hundred thousand board feet of pine lumber, shingles, and shakes at Grays Harbor, Washington, *Reporter* sailed for San Francisco in early March 1902. The crew grumbled about two bad omens: the ship sailed on a Friday, traditionally considered bad luck, and the ship's cat — who happened to be black — leaped overboard and drowned an hour before *Reporter* weighed anchor. The cook, a superstitious man, felt that "the poor thing committed suicide" rather than sail on a doomed ship.

On the evening of March 13 *Reporter* neared the Golden Gate in a thick fog. In the dark, Capt. Adolph Hansen saw a strong light to starboard, which he took to be the lighthouse at Point Bonita. Allowing the vessel to drive ahead and pass the light to enter the Gate, Hansen found himself caught in the surf; "not until the schooner was in the breakers did he know he was trying to hurdle her over the peninsula instead of going in orderly through the harbor entrance." Hansen mistook a light at the Cliff House for Point Bonita Light, and *Reporter* struck Ocean Beach about three miles south of Point Lobos, beaching where the bark *King Philip* had gone ashore in 1878.

Curious crowds gather around the broken hull of Aberdeen *on Ocean Beach.*

Heavy seas swept the decks, forcing the crew up into the rigging. The mizzen-mast fell, injuring one man who fell to the deck. Capt. Hansen had meanwhile flashed a light as a distress signal, alerting a surfman from the Golden Gate Life-Saving Station who was patrolling the beach. Rescuers soon arrived and launched a surfboat to retrieve *Reporter*'s crew. The surfboat swamped on the first attempt, but on the second try the crew was saved. Waves gradually pushed *Reporter* up on the beach, and by daylight the ship lay on its starboard side a hundred yards from shore. "During the day she heaved and lurched until she was lying almost stern on." According to the San Francisco *Examiner:*

> *There is no hope for the* Reporter. *Her cargo of lumber, worth $14,000, is likely to drift to the beach in parcels. It can be stacked and carted away into the city and so saved. The schooner can only fight till her tendons give. Her ribs and sheathing, masts and rails will wash ashore, to be carried away by thrifty seaside dwellers and be used as firewood.*

The schooner was visited by Capt. Hansen and the life-savers the day after the wreck, and the chronometer and a few personal effects were saved. Thousands of San Francisco residents visited the wreck, "and not even the biting wind and sudden squalls could keep them away." Enterprising businessmen posted broadsides on the hulk, advertising "Jesse Moore Rye and Bourbon" and "Boise Liniment" for rheumatism. The keel broken, *Reporter* began to fall apart and disappear beneath the sand, "fast digging her own grave alongside the bones of the *King Philip*, whose ribs are still seen. . . ."

Gifford
September 25, 1903

The 2245-ton steel, four-masted bark *Gifford* was built at Greenock, Scotland, by Scott & Co. in 1892, during a boom in large deepwaterman construction in the last decade of the nineteenth century occasioned by California grain and lumber and coal trade with Australia. The bark was destined for the Pacific. By 1895 *Gifford* was on the Pacific Coast, working in the lumber trade under British Registry. One newspaper account noted "The British iron [sic] ship *Gifford* . . . is operated by J.J. Moore & Company in the lumber trade between the Pacific Coast and Australia. She generally loads at San Francisco and the redwood portion of her cargo is taken to her by the schooners. She carries coal on the return trip from Australia." The ship was returning to San Francisco with coal from Newcastle, New South Wales on September 25, 1903.

As *Gifford* approached the Golden Gate that fateful day, a thick fog obscured the shore. Capt. Robert Michie, who had "only a vague idea that San Francisco was near . . . plowed ahead, with shortened sails, hearing and seeing no warnings." At 6 p.m. the ship struck the shore just off Mussel Rock, twelve miles south of Point Lobos. The crew reached shore safely after midnight as the heavy surf abated, and by the next morning help arrived. Tugs attempted to pull the bark free, but the hawsers parted. Holed and half submerged, the vessel was abandoned. Salvors stripped as much equipment and rigging as possible, and landed a portion of the coal cargo. Two weeks later, *Gifford* disintegrated in the surf. "The fate of the vessel was sealed yesterday when the battering waves reduced her sides to a shapeless mass of twisted iron and her heavily sparred mast was sent crashing over the side. . . . The hull has settled deep in the sands and only her torn and shattered bulwarks appear above water at high tide."

Capt. Michie's loss of the ship was inexcusable. Poor navigation had piled his ship onto the rocks because he had sailed ahead in fog without taking soundings. The British Consul in San Francisco quickly convened a court of inquiry, found the captain at fault, and stripped him of his master's license.

The steam schooner Yosemite, *capsized off Point Reyes, was wrecked on Ocean Beach as salvors vainly tried to tow the ship into San Francisco Bay.*

The Yosemite.

Aberdeen
June 23, 1916

The 499-ton steam schooner *Aberdeen* was built at Aberdeen, Washington in 1899 by J. Lindstrom. A single-ended steam schooner, *Aberdeen* was powered by a 425-horsepower compound engine. Built for the Pacific Lumber Company, *Aberdeen* carried passengers and up to five hundred thousand board feet of lumber on coastwise voyages. The steam schooner's lumber trade career ended in 1911 when it was sold to Fred Linderman of San Francisco. In conjunction with Linderman's steam schooner *Signal*, *Aberdeen* hauled barges of garbage from Oakland out the Golden Gate and dumped the loads off the Farallones — a controversial move, as the garbage occasionally floated ashore to litter San Francisco and San Mateo County beaches.

Alternately running three times a week to dump their loads twenty-five miles off the Golden Gate, *Aberdeen* and *Signal* operated without incident until 1913, when heavy seas on the bar claimed *Signal* and several crewmembers. *Aberdeen* shared *Signal*'s fate. On January 23, 1916, nearing the Golden Gate after dumping a load of garbage, *Aberdeen* encountered rough seas that capsized and broke up the ship. Several of the crew, including Capt. Knudson, drowned. Within a few days, most of *Aberdeen*'s shattered hull came ashore along a three-mile stretch of Ocean Beach. Timbers attracted curious onlookers before disappearing beneath the sand.

Yosemite
February 9, 1926

The 827-ton, single-ended steam schooner *Yosemite* was built by the Bendixsen Shipbuilding Company at Fairhaven, California in 1906. *Yosemite* was powered by a 750-horsepower, triple expansion engine manufactured by the Fulton Iron Works of San Francisco. Built for the Yosemite Steamship Company, a "single-ship corporation" of San Francisco, *Yosemite* carried passengers and 850,000 board feet of lumber on her coastwise voyages. In 1916 Pope and Talbot of San Francisco, the largest lumber firm on the Pacific Coast, purchased *Yosemite* to add to the company fleet. The steam schooner proved a good investment, showing "an annual profit of $15,000 during the ten years she operated" for Pope and Talbot. For the remainder of its career, *Yosemite* ran between San Francisco and the Pope and Talbot sawmills at Port Ludlow, Washington.

Steaming out of San Francisco on February 6, 1926, *Yosemite* carried twenty-five tons of dynamite. Just after midnight on February 7, *Yosemite* was off Point Reyes in a thick fog when it hit the rocks below Point Reyes light, tearing a hole in the bow. As Capt. Silvia backed off the rocks, *Yosemite* began to flood. The radio operator broadcast a distress signal, which was picked up by the steam schooner *Willamette* only five miles away. *Willamette* rescued *Yosemite*'s crew, who had taken to the boats and headed back for San Francisco. The Red Stack tug *Sea Ranger*, dispatched by Pope and Talbot, ran a hawser to *Yosemite*, whose starboard side was submerged, and began to tow it toward the Golden Gate. The task was difficult —

waves constantly washed over *Yosemite* and the hawser snapped once.

After a day-long battle with the sea, *Sea Ranger* arrived at the San Francisco Bar around 2 in the morning on February 8, towing the water-logged *Yosemite*. The derelict began to drift, and the tug, with all engines going full speed ahead, was pulled astern. The anchor was dropped and torn away, and at 3:15 *Yosemite* broke free and went adrift. Fifteen minutes later, *Yosemite* crashed ashore on Ocean Beach, breaking apart on the beach at the foot of Fulton Street,

just below the Cliff House. There was some speculation that the steam schooner's dynamite cargo had exploded, although the tug's crew reported that *Yosemite* had fallen apart. "Whatever the cause, the ship was splintered to atoms. Her wreckage, a litter of shattered timbers, empty powder boxes and broken spars, dotted the beach from the foot of Fulton Street to Fleishhacker Pool. Huge posts were twisted and spars were reduced to splinters."

Thousands of spectators crowded the beach for the next few days, picking up souvenirs and posing for

The freighter Ohioan *stranded and bilged at Point Lobos.*

pictures amid the wreckage. The largest surviving piece, *Yosemite*'s hull, drifted ashore bottom up, smashing into the Lurline Pier at the foot of Fulton Street. The pier, which held an intake pipe for San Francisco's saltwater Lurline Baths, was battered by the hulk until 250 feet of the pier was torn away. Workers gradually cleared the beach of smaller debris, but a week after the wreck, large sections of *Yosemite*'s hull remained visible.

Ohioan
October 7, 1936

The 5,153-ton freighter *Ohioan* was built in 1914 by the Maryland Steel Company at Sparrows Point, Maryland. The steel-hulled freighter was propelled by a four thousand-horsepower triple-expansion steam engine. *Ohioan* was built for American-Hawaiian Steamship Company of New York, a company established in 1899 and the most important American shipping firm of the early twentieth century. As owners of 25 percent of the deadweight tonnage of large U.S.-registered sea-going freighters in 1917, American-Hawaiian had revived the American merchant marine. It pioneered the American building of large, modern steam freighters, and oil-fired boilers, opened the combination steamer-railroad link across Mexico's Isthmus of Tehuantepec, and consistently earned profits. Its fleet of steamers, operating between the Atlantic and Pacific coasts and the Territory of Hawaii, "constituted the largest single fleet of freighters under the American flag." *Ohioan* was part of a major expansion of American-Hawaiian Steamship

Company between 1910 and 1915, when it doubled its fleet.

Ohioan operated on the Atlantic through 1920. During the First World War it was requisitioned by the United States government on America's entry in the war in 1917. American-Hawaiian's contribution to the war effort was significant. The first American troops sent to Europe in June 1917 went in the American-Hawaiian freighters *Dakotan* and *Montanan*, and 625,641 tons of cargo and 125,449 troops were carried in the company's steamers (including *Ohioan*) in 145 round-trip voyages. Five of the company's vessels were torpedoed and lost. At war's end the company resumed its operations, and *Ohioan* was the first to initiate intercoastal voyages, steaming from Boston to San Francisco in December 1920. For the remainder of its career, *Ohioan* steamed from coast to coast via the Panama Canal.

Bound for San Francisco with a load of washing machines, trucks, and general merchandise, *Ohioan* had picked up a pilot and was navigating through thick fog on October 7, 1936. Lost in the fog, Capt. Read and Pilot McFarland allowed the ship to swing too close to shore. Narrowly missing Seal Rocks, *Ohioan* sailed past the Cliff House and struck the rocks at Point Lobos at 11:20 p.m. Sparks from the steel hull's impact lit up the night sky. The engines were disabled, and No. 1 hold, open to the sea, flooded. Lying north of Sutro Baths in a small cove adjacent to Point Lobos, *Ohioan* lay one hundred yards from shore, starboard side to shore and the bow pointing northward.

The next day salvage of the cargo began. Tugs dispatched to pull *Ohioan* free could not reach the ship, "defeated by the heavy fog and treacherous

Ohioan's steel hull split open and breaking up, October 1939.

rocks," and a breeches buoy was finally rigged to carry some of the crew and cargo ashore on October 9. The next day barges moored against the ship to load large and heavy cargo. "Plunder cargo" or smaller packages were taken out and sent to shore on the breeches buoy. The San Francisco *Call-Bulletin* reported, "Whether the ship can be floated off will be determined only after most of the cargo is taken off and after divers have surveyed the damage."

Crowds of several thousand watched over the next week as fourteen hundred tons of cargo was taken out of *Ohioan* despite heavy swells and seas crashing against the ship's stern. American-Hawaiian Steamship Company wrote off the vessel as a total loss. On November 4, 1936, *Ohioan* was sold at closed-bid auction for $2,800.20 to William Mitchell of San Francisco. The vessel had originally cost $729,000. Mitchell's seven-month salvage of *Ohioan*'s remaining cargo and gear was a frustrating though ultimately rewarding experience. In December, Mitchell's barge *Ellen F.*, while moored next to *Ohioan*, broke free of its moorings and stranded on the beach near the Cliff House, but was pulled off. On March 6, 1937, the vessel was set ablaze when one of Mitchell's men torched spoiled meat in the hold. The flames spread to oil-soaked ropes and sacks and threatened to set off dynamite the salvors left on board, which would have ignited nine thousand gallons of crude oil in a fuel bunker. Mitchell and Joseph Rosenberg made several trips to the burning wreck to throw the dynamite overboard and quench the fire.

On June 29, 1937, Mitchell reported that he had sold *Ohioan* to a San Francisco scrap metal combine, who would cut up the wrecked freighter, which had been "stripped of all removable machinery, cargo, and furnishings. . ." The vessel was not scrapped, however, despite a "vigorous campaign" by the San Francisco Chamber of Commerce to clear the harbor entrance of the rusting hulks of *Ohioan* and *Frank H. Buck*. Nature finally obliged the Chamber of Commerce, with a winter storm in January 1938 bringing high tides that destroyed *Ohioan*. "Heavy surf, lashed by high winds, raged through the wreck of the steamer *Ohioan* at the Golden Gate, breaking the stern from the vessel and leaving the hull in three pieces as it was driven high on the beach."

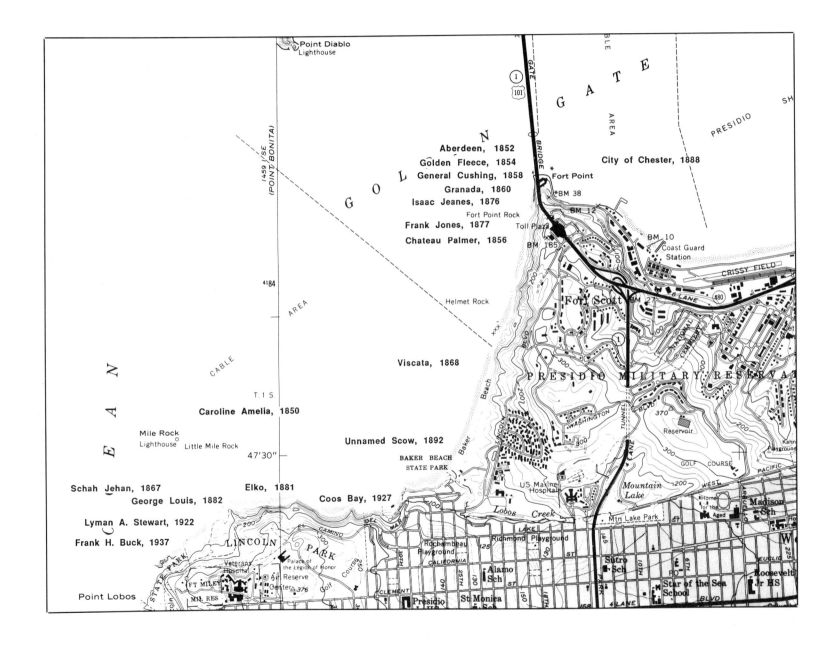

Chapter 3
Shipwrecks Of The San Francisco Headlands And The Golden Gate

The San Francisco headlands form a wide bight to the south of the entrance to the Golden Gate.

The San Francisco shoreline curves in a broad crescent north of Point Lobos along the cliffs and rocky shore stretching to Land's End before sweeping northwest to the Gate. The craggy coast is interrupted only by the sandy strands of China Beach and Baker Beach. Swift tides create navigational challenges. Offshore loom the Mile Rocks, another hazard to vessels approaching the harbor entrance from the south. Because of the very heavy vessel traffic in this area, shipwrecks have been frequent since gold rush times, and continue unabated into the twentieth century. Some of the most visible shipwrecks of modern times have taken place on the rocks around Land's End.

The Golden Gate is a mile wide. Here, at the drowned river channel of the Sacramento, tidal currents have cut a 340-foot deep canyon that drops abruptly from the two points that mark the Gate, Fort Point and Lime Point. Caution at this narrow entrance has limited the wrecks to a handful. Yet the wrecks at the Golden Gate contain the greatest number of fatalities because the wreck of *City of Rio de Janeiro* in February 1901 accounted for 228 lives, and the ramming and sinking of the steamer *City of Chester* in 1886 took over forty lives.

Caroline Amelia
March 19, 1850

Little is known about the career or wreck of the Danish bark *Caroline Amelia*, beyond its demise on Mile Rocks on March 19, 1850. A short account that appeared in the *Alta California* the next day, describes the incident:

> *Danish bark* Caroline Amelia, *which cleared on the 16th inst. for Costa Rica, was wrecked on the Mile Rocks in the offing yesterday morning. She was running for "the needles" when the breeze suddenly died away and a strong ebb tide set her in shore. She dropped anchors but her chain cables parted, and, in spite of all the exertions of the officers and crew she was driven by force of the current directly upon the above named rocks, staving an ugly hole in her bottom. Being an old ship her timbers soon*

gave way and filling steadily she went down in about ten fathoms of water, entirely out of sight. The captain succeeded in getting his chronometers, instruments, clothes, and money out of the ship before she sunk, and the crew saved all their dunnage.

Caroline Amelia may have been intending to pick up a load of gold-seekers who were crossing the isthmus of Central America on their way to California. The reference to Costa Rica, and the fact that there is no mention of cargo or passengers southbound, in the *Alta's* story make this a likely conjecture.

Aberdeen
December 1852

The 718-ton ship *Aberdeen* was built at Warren, Maine in 1847. *Aberdeen* was solely employed as a packet ship, sailing from New York to Liverpool. In 1847 the ship was one of two vessels inaugurating the "Sturges and Clearman Line" of New York. The following year *Aberdeen* sailed for "Slate's Liverpool Line" of packets. By 1851, the ship was a coastal packet connecting New York and Mobile for the "City Line" of Sturges and Clearwater. Sometime in 1852 *Aberdeen* sailed to California. The circumstances of the wreck in late December 1852 or early January 1853 are not recorded, but the log of the United States Revenue Marine cutter *Frolic* noted the wreck lay at the Golden Gate "ashore on the Rock off Fort Pt." On January 8, Capt. Douglass Ottinger boarded the wreck "and found her broken into two upon the rocks." By January 9, 1853 the wreck

had gone to pieces, and *Frolic* landed a crew to "save property" for the owners: thirteen hams, five pieces of pork, a keg of butter, and a box of soap were salvaged.

The vessel evidently stayed on the rocks at Fort Point for some time, for on February 16, 1854, the California Legislature passed a joint resolution instructing California's Congressional delegation to "obtain an appropriation from Congress, if possible, sufficient to procure the removal of the wreck of the ship *Aberdeen*, which now lies at the entrance of the Bay of San Francisco, and presents a serious obstruction to commerce." Part of the reason may have been the near-wreck of the tug *Goliah* on March 7, 1853, returning from San Francisco with passengers from the wrecked steamer *Tennessee*. Coming in, *Goliah* came too close to the shore at the Golden Gate and struck the submerged hulk of *Aberdeen*. Fortunately, the steamer passed safely over the wreck and saved *Tennessee's* passengers from a second shipwreck.

Golden Fleece
April 22, 1854

The 968-ton clipper ship *Golden Fleece* was built by Paul Curtis at Boston, Massachusetts in 1852. Constructed for Boston merchant William F. Weld and Co., the ship capsized while being rigged, definitely a bad omen. *Golden Fleece* sailed from Boston on August 16, 1852 for its maiden voyage to San Francisco. After a difficult passage, the clipper arrived at San Francisco 140 days later with eleven passengers and a speculative gold rush-era cargo of liquor, hardware, preserved foodstuffs, and "assorted goods."

Golden Fleece returned to the East Coast, sailing for Boston via Manila. She then sailed from New York for San Francisco a second time, arriving at the Golden Gate on April 10, 1854 after a 128-day passage. Twelve days later *Golden Fleece* departed San Francisco for Manila, but wrecked when beating out of the Golden Gate. Caught in an eddy, the ship missed stays and drifted ashore outside the gate at Fort Point. The next day found the clipper "lying broadside on to the rocks . . . bilged and full of water, her mainmast is gone, also the fore and main top mast." The tugs *Resolute* and *Hercules* attempted to pull *Golden Fleece* from the rocks and failed. By April 24 the salvage of the vessel was underway, the tug *Resolute* taking away "two loads of sails and rigging. . . ." The ship lay "stern on, all her masts gone, save the stump of the mainmast." Rumors along the waterfront blamed a drunken captain and a short-handed crew. The editors of the San Francisco *Daily Alta California* attacked the rumors in their April 25 edition, claiming, "It seems to have been the result of one of those class of accidents which happen even to the most careful and prudent."

The wreck of *Golden Fleece* was sold at public auction on April 24, 1854 to Silas E. Burrows and several other San Franciscans for $2,600. Over the next few days they worked to strip and lighten the vessel:

The purchasers of the wreck are busily engaged stripping her of everything moveable, at the same time preparations are being made to raise her. They hope to be successful, and from their present expectations may possibly succeed. The

Viscata *was wrecked due to pilot error just outside the gate on March 7, 1868.*

sails, rigging, guns, & c., saved by the consignee of the ship, were sold at auction yesterday, the two brass pieces bringing $580.

The salvors sent three hundred men to strip the wreck in late April, but four were drowned on May 1 when their boat capsized in the surf as they headed from the shore to the wreck. Only one man in the boat survived. Six days later, the papers noted that all efforts to salvage the wreck off the rocks had ceased, since "the parties who purchased her have stripped her of everything moveable, and now await the time she may break up for further gain." The last mention of the wreck of *Golden Fleece* was made by Thomas Boyd, a passenger who had sailed in the ship on her maiden voyage to San Francisco. Writing to his daughter on May 15, Boyd said he had visited the wreck; "Notwithstanding that her strong sides stood the beating of the angry billows, and her tall masts stood through the fury of the gale — she now lies a helpless wreck, on the rocks, not more than a cable's length from the shore." Boyd lamented, "She has been clear round the world, since she landed me here. I went on board her several times while she was discharging [cargo] & everything looked so familiar. I cannot help feeling some sense of sorrow at her loss."

Chateau Palmer
May 1, 1856

The eight hundred-ton ship *Chateau Palmer* of Le Havre, France was lost on the return leg of its maiden voyage when it missed stays and crashed ashore at Fort Point on May 1, 1856. The voyage began when the ship arrived at San Francisco in early 1856 with a "full cargo of merchandise," and was chartered by the firm of Bolton, Barron and Forbes, operators of California's New Almaden mercury mines, to ship 719 flasks of quicksilver from San Francisco to Callao, Peru. The New Almaden Mines, some fifty miles south of San Francisco and near San Jose, were in the process of being developed into North America's principal supplier of mercury; the quicksilver carried aboard *Chateau Palmer* was not only a cargo representing the diversity and richness of California in the first years after the gold rush as attention turned from gold to other commodities; the flasks of mercury were among the millions that would bring wealth to the mines' owners and operators for nearly a century. Departing San Francisco on May 1, 1856, *Chateau Palmer* was just outside the Golden Gate when lost:

In attempting to wear ship, finding that she would not clear the shore, both anchors were immediately let go, when she dragged ashore about five hundred yards west of Fort Point. The wind blowing fresh from the WNW at the time, with a heavy sea running, she struck heavily. Immediately after striking, she floated off shore with the head to the westward.

Three days later, a summary of the fortnight's news noted that the ship, with a cargo of quicksilver and "China goods," had gone ashore and "became a total wreck, but the cargo was saved." No further mention of the wreck of *Chateau Palmer* was made.

The water pours over the bulwarks of the bark Gifford; Mussel Rock looms inshore of the wreck.

The ship Frank Jones, *hopelessly stranded off Baker Beach, March 30, 1877.*

General Cushing
October 16, 1858

The 681-ton ship *General Cushing* was built at Bath, Maine in 1856 and launched in January of 1857. Owned by Benjamin Dow, Nicholas Varina, Moses Hale, and Benjamin Davis of Newburyport, and Robert Morss of Boston, *General Cushing* was commanded by Varina. It was common practice for masters to be part owners of their ships. On September 3, 1858, the vessel arrived at San Francisco from Australia to load grain. After lying at the Lombard Street Wharf for two weeks loading ten thousand bags of oats and ten thousand bags of barley, *General Cushing* sailed from San Francisco for Sydney on October 16, 1858.

In company with the clipper *War Hawk* and several other vessels, *General Cushing* was just past the Golden Gate at twenty minutes to one in the afternoon when the ship missed stays. Failing to make one last tack to beat out past the Gate, *General Cushing* was caught in the ebbing tide. The anchors were dropped but did not hold, and the ship swung into the rocks at Fort Point, "at a point about midway between where the *Golden Fleece. . . .* and the *Chateau Palmer. . .* were wrecked, and just under the 'ten gun battery' on the hill." The vessel lay close in to shore, rocking violently in the surf and striking on the bottom. The masts were cut away to reduce the strain on the hull. The wreck was described the following day as "a mere mass of timber festooned with broken spars and tangled rigging. . . . at times portions of her keel rolled up to the surface of the water; the mangled stumps of

the masts projected out of the decks, and the bowsprit and jibboom were draped in ragged masses of canvas."

On October 17 salvage of the cargo commenced. "Three lighter loads of merchandise were removed from the ship *General Cushing*. . . . The ship lies in the same position, and as the wind has gone down which blew so strongly . . . she does not thump as heavily as she did. The next gale will probably break her up." On the following day, the wreck and cargo of *General Cushing* were sold at auction by McRuer and Merrill of San Francisco. The sale price was not recorded. Although most of the cargo was pulled from the vessel, *General Cushing* was a total loss.

Granada
October 13, 1860

The 1,058-ton side-wheel steamship *Granada* was built by Jeremiah Simonson at New York in 1855. *Granada* was propelled by side-wheels driven with a vertical-beam steam engine. *Granada* carried passengers between New York and Panama for the United States Mail Steamship Company from 1857 to 1859, shifting in early 1860 to the run between New York and New Orleans. *Granada* came to grief in January 1860 on striking floating ice on the Hudson River. After an anxious race to New York, the steamer sank at the dock, leaving only the bow sticking up out of the water. The following day, as steam pumps labored to raise the sunken steamer, one of the boilers burst, killing a deck hand and scalding several others. The boiler flew twenty feet into the air, landing on *Granada*'s pilothouse. *Granada* was finally raised and repaired. The owner, Marshall O. Roberts, president of the United States Mail Steamship Company, then decided to send the steamship through the Straits of Magellan into the Pacific. *Granada* was intended as the first steamer on a steamship line to link San Francisco with the East Coast by means of a land route across Mexico's Isthmus of Tehuantepec. *Granada* would run in tandem with the steamer *Moses Rogers.*

Arriving off the Golden Gate on October 13, 1860, *Granada* took aboard a pilot and was slowly working through the thick fog when the main steam line broke, disabling the engine and scalding the chief engineer. Without power, the steamer drifted into the surf, grounding on a sandbar near Fort Point beach five hundred yards south of the fort. "The surf ran violently and broke with great force against the sides." A crewmember swam ashore with a line, and with assistance from shore, linked ship to shore. For the next few days crowds flocked to Fort Point to see the beached steamer. "At the last flood tide, she was drifted far up, and yesterday she was but a few yards from high water mark." The sternpost broke away, seams opened, and the steamer gone. *Granada* lay in nine feet of water with the tide ebbing and flowing into the hull.

The wreck was a popular attraction. The San Francisco *Daily Alta California* of October 15, 1860 noted, "The *Granada* was visited by crowds of people yesterday, as she lay high and dry beyond Fort Point." The wreck could not be pulled free. On October 18 "the hull of the Steamship *Granada* . . . together with her engine, boilers, & c., including everything that may be on board" was sold at auction. The California Steam Navigation Company purchased the wreck for $2,600.

Within a few days, "men . . . were taking the machinery out, and assisting the waves to break to pieces what is left of her." After removing the engines and boilers, they abandoned the stripped hulk to the surf.

The wreck was blamed on the lack of a fog signal at Point Bonita. The first fog signal on the Pacific Coast of the United States, a small 24-pdr. flank howitzer, was emplaced at the point in 1855, but the difficulty of firing the gun constantly every twenty minutes in day after day of thick fog led to its abandonment. In a letter signed "Fog-Gun," a reader exhorted his fellows:

> *Shall we wait until a passenger laden ship is piled up at our very doors, and listen to the shrieks of the doomed wretches before we bestir ourselves in this matter of humanity? Reader, have you a wife, sister, or child coming in the Golden Gate? You owe them a duty to put your shoulder to this wheel, and heave with a will. . . . To all we put the direct question, will it be easier to get this gun to work again, or to bury the drowned. . . .*

The fog gun was not put back into commission, but officials did order fog horns at Point Bonita and a fog bell installed at Fort Point. Other aids to navigation at the Gate followed, but were not enough to forestall the inevitable. The grim prophecy of 1860 was realized forty-one years later when the passenger-laden steamer *City of Rio de Janeiro* struck at the Gate and sank with the shrieks of victims resounding through the fog.

Frank Jones, *bilged and on the rocky beach near Fort Point.*

Schah Jehan
February 3, 1867

Schah Jehan (or Shah Jehan) was a British full-rigged ship. Termed an "old vessel" on arrival in San Francisco, *Schah Jehan*'s origins and career are unknown. The ship carried a cargo of coal, tobacco, and brandy from Sydney, Australia. A customs collector seized the cargo, and arrested the captain and mate for smuggling. Released on bond, they departed San Francisco "rather hurriedly" on the afternoon of February 3, 1867, bound, it was stated, "up the Coast for lumber." It was conjectured that "this haste to leave [within] two weeks probably caused the loss of the vessel."

The *Alta California* stated that the immediate cause of the wreck was "missing stays through the breaking of the mainsail sheet." The ship had probably departed short-handed, a primary cause of "missing stays." *Schah Jehan* was driven ashore between Point Lobos and the South Head, where the bottom was stove in. All aboard reached shore safely. Salvors bought the wreck shortly thereafter, but it broke up before any work could take place. "A cleaner break-up and disappearance we never saw in our life." One wonders if the accused smugglers ever stood trial, or if they disappeared as well.

Viscata
March 7, 1868

Viscata was launched in Liverpool, England in 1864, a staunchly built iron-hulled vessel that Lloyd's of London gave its highest rating during surveys in Liverpool and San Francisco. Referred to as both a bark and a ship, photographs taken at the site of the vessel's stranding clearly show it crossing a square yard for a mizzen course, and therefore *Viscata* was rigged as a ship at the time of loss. Owner J. Steel of Liverpool engaged the ship in a deep-water trade that took it more than once to San Francisco Bay to load cargoes of California grain, probably in exchange for manufactured goods from England.

On March 7, 1868 *Viscata* cleared North Point and stood out the Golden Gate on an ebb tide. Capt. Drummond was the master, but the ship was under the direction of the port pilot, Capt. Jolliff, who had recently been in charge of the ill-fated ship *Oliver Cutts*, wrecked off Alcatraz only fifty-five days before. The wind was coming out of the northwest, and the ship commenced beating out the narrow harbor entrance, tacking once off Fort Point, again off the Sausalito side, and attempted to do so a third time near the Fort again.

On the last attempt, the wind shifted suddenly to the north. *Viscata* missed stays and was taken aback

The scow schooner Elko, trapped in the rocks of Lands End, April 26, 1881.

just as it came dangerously close to the frothing rip of a counter-current. While moving astern, the crew dropped the starboard anchor and ran out sixty fathoms of chain, in an attempt to bring the vessel's head into the wind. The fates conspired against *Viscata*, however, for the anchor stock broke and the anchor failed to hold. It was now too late to avoid grounding — even if the ship had let go a second anchor, it would have run over the chain. *Viscata* came up broadside on the sands of Baker Beach, where successive waves pushed it higher and higher, until beachcombers could walk up and touch the hull.

The tug *Rescue* tried to pull the vessel free on the high tide but failed, and the hulk was sold at auction to Messrs. Stevens, Baker & Co. for $22,500 in gold. The prevailing calm weather, as well as the vessel's position embedded in soft sand, created a general feeling that "there is a big thing in the purchase of the vessel, as she is lying, at the price paid." The cargo of 32,731 one hundred-pound sacks of wheat was, however, sold to separate parties, and therein the vessel's fate was sealed.

The coastal steamer City of Chester *steamed between San Francisco and Eureka until wrecked in 1888.*

The vessel owners, busily stripping *Viscata's* topmasts, rigging, and spars, and pumping the hold dry, refused at first to allow the cargo owners to remove sacks of wheat. Although much of the cargo was eventually removed from the hull in an effort to lighten ship and float it free, the efforts came too late. When a heavy storm came up, both parties lost out as the vessel went to pieces.

The newspapers accounts stated dramatically:

The scene at the time was magnificent — the huge rollers, coming in with military precision and regularity, lifting their crests with a mighty roar and hurling themselves upon the fated ship, as if determined to destroy her utterly, while the sea and shore were strewn with her timbers, deck planking, and such portions of her cargo as had not yet been taken from her. Notwithstanding the rain that poured down unceasingly, many persons rode out from the city to witness the scene, and the bluff and the beach were covered at times with spectators.

In the end, *Viscata*:

Worked loose from her bed of sand, and somewhat farther inshore, when her wooden decks began to yield to the tremendous blows of the waves, and gradually broke up as the beams were broken and timbers twisted and split to pieces. With the deck gone and the hold filled with water, the waves had full sweep. The iron plates on her starboard side near the bow and stern began to yield. The seams along the bilge began to open also, and the mainmast, with the iron maintopmast, fell out and went over the side to seaward, while the port side of the hull succumbed to the pressure and curled in "like a burnt shoe." The iron foremast was also bent and broken, threatening to fall at any moment. The mizzenmast alone stood erect and appeared uninjured . . . At nightfall only the ragged and torn shell of iron was left to tell of the magnificent ship. . . .

The Pilot Examiners revoked the pilot's license, despite supportive testimony by Capt. Drummond of *Viscata*. The examiners reasoned that he should not have attempted to come about so close to an obvious back eddy, and that more efforts should have been made to let go a second anchor.

Issac Jeanes
March 9, 1876

The 814-ton bark *Isaac Jeanes* was built in 1854 at Philadelphia, Pennsylvania. Launched from the yard of William Cramp into the Delaware River, the bark was originally rigged as a ship and was one of only four clipper ships built at Philadelphia. Constructed for the Isaac Jeanes Company, *Isaac Jeanes* was a clipper packet in the Mediterranean trade that made "one run in the California trade during the clipper ship decade—a passage of 129 days in 1855." In 1854 *Isaac Jeanes* served for a short time on the "Black Diamond Line" of packets between Philadelphia and Liverpool and on the "New Orleans Packet Line" that connected that southern city to Philadelphia. By 1874 the vessel was operating out of San Francisco.

On March 9, 1876 *Isaac Jeanes*, inbound with a cargo of lumber, wrecked at the Golden Gate near Fort Point. The bark was entering the harbor "with a westerly breeze, the wind suddenly came out from the easterly, and after a vain attempt to tack ship, but not having room, she went ashore . . . near the spot where the steamer *Granada* was lost." The crew barely escaped as the vessel broke up in the surf immediately after striking. "There was not a vestige of her to be seen, excepting a few spars and some rigging, the cargo of lumber having drifted in and out the harbor in all directions." There was no further mention of *Isaac Jeanes*.

Frank Jones
March 30, 1877

The ship *Frank Jones* was a fine example of the New England shipbuilder's art. Launched in 1874, the first-class vessel was built very strongly of oak, and given the highest Lloyd's ratings for wooden ships. A downeaster built to carry large cargos on lengthy voyages, *Frank Jones* twice went from New York to San Francisco to Liverpool and back. The third voyage was never completed. On the second voyage *Frank Jones* made passage from New York to San Francisco in 126 days. On March 30, 1877 the downeaster left port under the command of Capt. James N. Nickles, bound for Manila in ballast. With a fresh gale blowing from the west-northwest and a pilot on board, *Jones* proceeded out the Golden Gate towed in the wake of the powerful tug *Monarch*.

The liner Oceanic *ramming and sinking* City of Chester *off Fort Point on the foggy morning of August 22, 1888.*

Monarch chose a course close to the south shore and passed Fort Point by "a cable's length . . . not only an objectionable, but a dangerous course, with the wind as it was. . . ." Just past the fort, the hawser parted. The *Jones* began to make sail in an effort to gain steerageway—a task made doubly difficult in the strong wind by the empty vessel's high sides. As the tug came up, both skippers began to dicker over whose hawser to use. *Jones* finally passed over a spare, but it was old and rotten and soon parted. By now the vessel was in deep trouble. Anchors wouldn't hold in the deep waters and swift current, and the ship was blown out of control across the South Bight, where it struck the shore south of Fort Point. Scraping across sharp rocks, *Jones* wedged between the rocks and a small sandy beach and came to rest nearly upright. Soon the tug *Rescue* came up to assist *Monarch*, but both tugs hauling together could not budge the ship. The hull was torn to ribbons, the hold flooded with twelve feet of water.

The Board of Pilot Commissioners held an official inquiry that cleared the pilot and blamed the tug's captain, since the towed vessel at the time was under the control of the tug's master. *Jones* was quickly sold at the Merchant's Exchange to Capt. Lees for $4,750. By then, a sand bar had formed out to the wreck, and curiosity-seekers could walk out "dry-shod" at low tide. As thousands came out to watch, Lees stripped the ship of stores, spars, and sails, and installed steam pumps in an attempt to work the wreck free and repair it. His hard work failed, and *Jones* was sold again to Col. A.W. Von Schmidt — this time for a mere $700. Schmidt tried to raise it farther up the beach and repair it there, but gave up and dismantled the wreck where it lay.

Elko
April 26, 1881

The 147-ton, two-masted scow schooner *Elko*, built in 1868 at San Francisco and "formerly owned and used as a coal scow by the Central Pacific Railroad Company," spent the last years of its career working in the Pacific Coast lumber trade. On April 26, 1881 *Elko*, loaded with lumber from Salmon Creek, California, crossed San Francisco Bar and was off the South Head (Point Lobos) when the outgoing tide caught the vessel and swept it in toward the rocks. Both anchors were let go, but *Elko* grounded near Pyramid Rock at Land's End, foundering in the surf. The tug *Wizard* tried to pull the scow schooner off, but was nearly lost after it came down on a submerged rock and had to return to San Francisco.

Two more tugs, *Rescue* and *Water Witch*, responded to the wreck and attached a line, but as *Rescue* pulled *Elko* free, the rocks sawed the rope and the schooner went ashore again, "where she remained all day, lying in a bad position and full of water." Late in the afternoon two more tugs, *Neptune* and *Monarch*, attempted to pull *Elko* off the rocks, but could not approach in the heavy surf, which by then was "making a clean breach over the vessel. . . . After waiting about two hours, they were compelled to give it up for a hopeless job."

George Louis
March 8, 1882

George Louis was a small two-masted, forty-ton coasting schooner built at San Francisco in 1863. While bound from San Francisco to Timber Cove, California on March 8, 1882 (presumably to load lumber), it went ashore inside Mile Rock, six and one-half miles northeast of the Golden Gate Park Life-Saving Station. Captain Erickson and the crew of three were saved, but the vessel, valued at $4,000, was a total loss.

The men of the Life-Saving Station responded to the wreck, and wrote their account of the incident:

It was impossible for the accident to be seen from the station, and the keeper was not aware of its occurrence until the fact was reported by a messenger from Captain John Low, of the Point Lobos Signal Station, who, upon discovering the vessel ashore, dispatched his son, John B.

Low, to the station, and then hurried to the spot alone to render assistance. The keeper immediately sent off for a team to draw the apparatus, and was soon on the way to the stranded vessel, arriving on the scene about 5 o'clock after a hard ride. By that time the captain and two others of the schooner's crew had managed, with the assistance of Captain Low, to climb the rocks and were safe, the cook, who was badly hurt by his efforts to make the ascent, being still at the foot of the cliff, unable to help himself. As young Low was the lightest man of the party he gallantly volunteered to make the descent and attach a line to the poor fellow so he could be hauled up. Accordingly, the young man was lowered over the precipice, a distance of seven hundred and eighty feet, by one of the station's lines, and upon reaching the foot of the cliff he bent a line around the man's body and he was safely hauled to the top. As he was unable to walk and in great pain, he was taken to the house of Captain Low, which was the nearest place of shelter, and was there properly cared for until the next day, when he was removed to San Francisco. The report of the district superintendent states that but for the timely arrival of the station appliances the man must soon have perished, the place where he was being a very dangerous one and inaccessible except by perilous descent from the top of the cliff, as undertaken by young Low. The vessel broke up during the night, and, on the following day scarcely a vestige of her was to be seen.

Young John Low, hero of the wreck, ironically later was shipwrecked himself when the schooner *Nettie Low* was lost below Double Point near Bolinas in February 1900.

City of Chester
August 22, 1888

Until the loss of *City of Rio de Janeiro* in 1901, the worst maritime disaster at the Golden Gate was the ramming and sinking of the iron-hulled coastal passenger liner *City of Chester* in 1888. The 1,106-ton steamer was built at Chester, Pennsylvania in 1875. Owned by the Pacific Coast Steamship Company, *City of Chester* operated along the coast, carrying passengers and freight between San Francisco and the lumbering ports on California's Humboldt Bay. Upon its first arrival at Eureka, California, the steamer was described as "the finest steamship ever in our harbor. . . . large and roomy, having the finest of accommodations for passengers." Trouble befell *City of Chester* in January 1886 when it ran aground on the South Spit of the Humboldt Bay Bar. The steamer was safely floated on the next high tide, but lost the rudder, rudder post, and a propeller blade.

City of Chester's luck ran out with the second accident. With passengers on board, the steamer departed San Francisco on the foggy morning of August 22, 1888. As *City of Chester* steamed past Fort Point, an incoming iron-hulled passenger liner, *Oceanic*, just arriving from Hong Kong and Yokohama, hit *Chester* at 9:25 a.m. The huge *Oceanic*

This stranded schooner is probably the 1888 wreck of Bessie Everding *on Ocean Beach.*

cut through *City of Chester*'s hull just forward of the stack on the port side, ripping a large gash "as clean as that made by a knife into cheese." *Oceanic* kept going, the momentum keeping the impaled *Chester* afloat long enough to allow several passengers to clamber aboard *Oceanic*. When the liner stopped, *City of Chester* slipped free. The stern lifted high into the air and the vessel sank rapidly, the boilers exploding as cold seawater hit hot metal. Taking sixteen passengers down, *City of Chester* plunged deep into the Golden Gate channel. Boats from *Oceanic* plucked about fifty survivors from the water, while other boats on the bay,

City of Rio de Janeiro *in the Orient. The 1901 wreck of the steamer, with 128 lives lost, was the worst maritime disaster at the Golden Gate.*

including the ferry *San Rafael*, rescued others.

Oceanic, though badly damaged, managed to stay afloat as members of the liner's crew leapt into the water to save the survivors from *City of Chester*. The wreck's location was marked by an oil slick that guided diver Victor Hinston to her. At fifty fathoms "he found the vessel lying across the channel cut in two. Water was rushing through the cut like a mill race." No attempt was made to salvage the wreck until 1890, when wrecker Thomas Whitelaw sounded the wreck. "It was discovered that the *City of Chester* lay on a sloping ledge with her bow in 40 fathoms of water and her stern in 46 fathoms. This depth was too great . . . and it is not probable that any attempt will be made to raise her." Capt. Thomas Wallace of *City of Chester* blamed the collision on the fog and the swift tides at the Golden Gate: "The tide caught us as we came nearer and swung our bow around. It was certainly not two minutes from the time we saw the *Oceanic* to the time she struck us. . . ." The heroes of the disaster were members of *Oceanic*'s Chinese crew, some of whom leapt into the water to save drowning passengers from *City of Chester*. A Board of Inquiry censured the pilot and Capt. Metcalfe of *Oceanic* for not stopping and backing the liner when they spotted *City of Chester* crossing their bow. Capt. Wallace of *Chester* was censured for not backing and stopping, and for not minding his helm in the strong tidal current. Pilot Meoyers and Capt. Metcalfe, who had been aboard a foreign flag vessel, were not subject to action by the United States Inspectors of Steamships. However, Capt. Wallace was, and lost his master's license for negligence.

Unnamed Scow

October 12, 1892

One wonders how many minor sinkings, strandings, fires, and other losses have happened that never made the historical record. One small incident that is noteworthy only because the story came to light took place on October 12, 1892, when an unnamed scow drifted ashore one and one-half miles south of the Fort

A Thousand Boys in Blue on S. S. Rio-de-Janeiro bound for Manila
Copyright 1898 by M. H. Z...

City of Rio carried American troops to the Philippines during the Spanish American War in 1898.

Point Life-Saving Station, and was totally wrecked. The vessel was valued at $1,500 and carried gear worth $500. A wire cable was run to a tugboat, which attempted in vain to haul the scow off. She was then stripped of everything of value that could be saved, including the tug's parted cable, in a process that took the salvors three days. No injuries occurred and no lives were lost, in this minor footnote to history.

City of Rio de Janeiro
February 22, 1901

The 3,548-ton iron-hulled steamship *City of Rio de Janeiro* was built in 1877-1878 at Chester, Pennsylvania by John Roach, the foremost marine engine manufacturer and shipbuilder in the United States in the late nineteenth century. *City of Rio de Janeiro* was laid down with its sister ship *City of Para*, to link Brazil with the United States. Launched on March 6, 1878, *City of Rio de Janeiro* was termed "a first class screw-steamer: "The ship is inclosed with iron from the stern up to the hurricane deck, aft of the fore-hatch, to give her extra strength. . . . The joiner work is . . . most splendid and elegant. . . . The *Rio de Janeiro* will accommodate 100 first-class passengers and about 500 in the steerage."

The steam line to Brazil was a failure. *City of Rio de Janeiro* proved particularly expensive: in 1879 the steamer ran down three ships, including the lightship at the mouth of the Amazon River, and sank two of the vessels. *City of Rio de Janeiro* and *City of Para* were sold in 1881 to the Pacific Mail Steamship Company of New York, which sent both vessels into service on the Panama route, *City of Para* on the Atlantic side, *City of Rio de Janeiro* on the Pacific side of the continent.

City of Rio de Janeiro made only one voyage to Panama before going into trans-Pacific service. For the remainder of its career, the steamer connected San Francisco with Honolulu, Yokohama, Japan, and Hong Kong. Although the steamer carried freight and well-to-do passengers, its most significant service was the transportation of thousands of immigrant Chinese to a new life in America. Its long career was eventful: frequently the vessel was involved in customs cases, as smugglers used *City of Rio de Janeiro* to bring a variety of items, usually opium, into the United States. In 1890 *City of Rio de Janeiro* was rammed by the English steamer *Bombay*, crushing the bow and forcing an eighteen-day delay in the next sailing. In January 1895 the steamer again met with accident when it ran aground on the rocks outside Nagasaki harbor.

The United States Army's Quartermaster Corps chartered *City of Rio de Janeiro* during the Spanish-American War as a troop transport. On July 22, 1898, the ship steamed from San Francisco with 888 men and 40 officers from the 1st South Dakota Infantry, the 1st and 2nd Battalions of the 18th U.S. Infantry, a Signal Corps detachment, and recruits for the Utah Light Artillery. Arriving at Manila on August 24, 1898, *City of Rio de Janeiro* was quickly made ready for a return voyage. Sailing on September 22, 1898, the steamer brought 150 sick and wounded soldiers back to San Francisco on October 22.

Returning to immigrant service in 1900, *City of Rio de Janeiro* made only a few voyages before it was lost in heavy fog on entering San Francisco Bay early

Wreck of the tanker Lyman Stewart, *aground at Lands End after being rammed by the freighter* Walter A. Luckenbach *on October 7, 1922.*

on the morning of February 22, 1901. Delayed two days by faulty machinery, the steamer arrived off the Golden Gate on the evening of February 21. Anchoring four miles to the west of Point Lobos and off the bar, *City of Rio de Janeiro* was hailed by the pilotboat *Gracie S.* at 5 p.m. Pilot Frederick Jordan, a master mariner with twelve years' experience as a bar pilot, climbed aboard the steamer to guide it into port. With Jordan in the pilothouse, *City of Rio de Janeiro* moved across the bar to anchor a mile off the Cliff House at 5:30 p.m. Marine Exchange lookout Capt. John Hyslop, from his wooden station atop Point Lobos, heard the steamer anchor for the night through the thick fog.

The next morning around 4 a.m., the anchor was raised and *City of Rio de Janeiro* proceeded in darkness and fog toward the Golden Gate. Lookout Hyslop at Point Lobos saw the steamer moving through the shifting fog. Aboard *Rio de Janeiro*, pilot Jordan and Capt. Ward were both anxious to make the Gate and San Francisco. Already delayed, and carrying an important passenger, U.S. Consul-General Rounceville Wildman, who was eager to catch a morning train in order to attend President William McKinley's inaugural ball in Washington, D.C., Capt. Ward and the pilot decided to press ahead. Slowly moving through the channel and toward the narrow Gate, the steamer was again enveloped by fog. The pilot did not stop the steamer nor return to anchorage, or apparently even order soundings to "feel" his way in, as prudence and experience should have dictated. Instead, *City of Rio de Janeiro* continued on course, striking the rocks at the Golden Gate without warning at 5:30 a.m. Pilot Jordan noted "the shock was so pronounced that I knew great damage had been done."

Bow view of the wrecked Lyman Stewart. *The tanker gradually broke apart; now only its engine is visible from the beach.*

Hung up on the rocks, *City of Rio de Janeiro* began to fill rapidly. Built to the standards of another era, the steamer did not have watertight bulkheads throughout the hull, and water freely flooded the ship. Three of the steamer's eleven boats were launched, but one was swamped, another crushed. Many passengers, asleep in their cabins at the time of the collision, never made it to the deck. Within three minutes of striking, the lights below deck failed, plunging those fighting their way to the deck in darkness. Therefore, most passengers remained below when the steamer slipped beneath the surface. In just ten minutes *City of Rio de Janeiro* backed off the rocks, drifted out with the ebb tide and sank. The ship took 128 of the 210 passengers and crew to a watery grave. Most of the 82 survivors were pulled from makeshift rafts and wreckage by fishing boats that arrived on the scene as they departed for the day's fishing. The passing of the steamer left a large amount of small debris on the water. "Small bits of broken planking strewed the vicinity of the wreck and floated with the changing tide, leaving a grewsome [sic] trail from Land's End up through Raccoon Straits to the Berkeley shores."

The vessel apparently sank intact and little floated up from the wreck save a few bodies and light flotsam. In July 1902 the pilothouse tore free from the submerged hulk and drifted ashore at Fort Baker inside the Gate. Inside the pilothouse, the badly decomposed corpse of *City of Rio de Janeiro*'s captain, William Ward, was found, still partially clad in his uniform. The captain was identified by his distinctive watch and its fob, a Chinese silver coin. The wreck of *City of Rio de Janeiro* was the worst maritime disaster off San Francisco's shores. Bitter condemnation of the Pacific

Mail Steamship Company, Capt. Ward and, to some extent, Pilot Jordan, continued for years. "This is the second large steamship [the first was the Pacific Mail steamer *City of New York* in 1893] lost within the Heads through a gross neglect to obey the promptings of sound seamanship."

The courts found that both Capt. Ward, who went down with his ship, and Pilot Jordan, who survived, had been grossly negligent in trying to enter the Golden Gate in the fog. The decision surprised no one. As early as April, 1901, Alexander Woolf, writing in the *Overland Monthly*, noted that "the most frequent cause of shipwreck on this coast is the neglect of taking soundings in thick and foggy weather; and this was the cause of unfortunate wrecking of the Rio." The pilot claimed that due to the depth of the channel and the heavy current it was impossible to take soundings. But damning evidence that it *was* possible because a patent sounding machine was aboard worked against Frederick Jordan's story. The courts also found Pacific Mail culpable—the decision of the United States District Court was that part of the blame for the heavy loss of life, but not the wreck, lay in the fact that the crew were Chinese and the officers white. Despite the proven competence of the crew, the court found that boats were separated, that the crew did not understand the language of the officers in command, that only two interpreters were aboard, and "therefore thought it not surprising that more boats were not lowered promptly and held the owners directly at fault for the inadequacy of the crew and liable in full for the loss." Survivors and family members of the victims received cash settlements in 1903 totalling $24,8267.93 by order of Judge DeHaven of the United States District Court.

Lyman A. Stewart

October 7, 1922

Lyman A. Stewart was built in 1914 at San Francisco's Union Iron Works. Named for the president and one of the founders of the Union Oil Company, *Lyman A. Stewart* was delivered to its owners ten months after its sister ship, *Frank H. Buck,* an identical steel-hulled oil tanker. In contrast to the *Buck's* constant adventures, *Lyman Stewart* had a quiet career in coastwise service on the West Coast, plying a regular route so uneventfully that the tanker was known as "the ol' lady" until lost.

Leaving the Union Oil Company's docks at the San Francisco Bay port of Oleum, heavy with oil bound for Seattle, *Lyman A. Stewart* approached the Golden Gate on the afternoon of October 7, 1922. Captain J.G. Cloyd was in command. A heavy swell and a strong tidal current added to the danger of a thick fog bank as the tanker proceeded out the harbor entrance along the northern, or outbound, side of the main ship channel.

At the same time the freighter *Walter A. Luckenbach* was heading in to the Gate at the end of a long voyage that began in New York. The fog muffled horns and whistles on both vessels. Capt. Brenner of *Luckenbach* saw the long hull of *Stewart* cut across his bow, and heard the blasts of its whistle — too late to avoid disaster. The freighter cut deep into the port bow of the heavily laden tanker, causing water to rush in and putting it down by the bow immediately. The *Stewart's* Captain Cloyd ordered hands to abandon ship, while he stayed with his command and piloted it toward shore, trailing oil. *Stewart* grounded on the

rocks at Land's End and ripped its hull on the jagged rocks. All thirty-eight hands aboard were saved.

In spite of strenuous efforts to float the tanker, *Lyman A. Stewart* remained hard aground. Eventually heavy seas picked up the hulk and jammed it farther up on the rocks, breaking it in two. In 1938 the wreck of *Stewart* and *Frank H. Buck,* which had wrecked at the same spot in 1937, were dynamited in an effort to clear the entrance of the harbor of visible wrecks. The hulks of both vessels slipped farther below the waves, where now only the engine block of *Stewart* protrudes at low tide.

Coos Bay

October 22, 1927

Coos Bay was laid down at Sparrow's Point, Maryland in 1909, and launched by the Maryland Steel Company under the name of *Vulcan.* A sister ship, *Cyclops,* later grained fame as a victim of the notorious "Bermuda Triangle." A steel-hulled vessel intended for service as a collier, *Vulcan* had a pilothouse forward of midships and additional superstructure aft. The Navy Department owned the ship and based it in Baltimore for coaling Navy vessels. For a long time the ship serviced various depots along the Eastern Seaboard including service in World War I. With oil steadily replacing coal as the fuel for modern vessels, *Vulcan* was sold out of naval service in 1924.

The Pacific States Lumber Company of Delaware bought the collier for use on the West Coast, converting it to a modern bulk carrier of lumber. The sale reflected the passing of the generation of wooden-

Coos Bay, *bow torn free, on the rocks near China Beach where the freighter stranded in October 1929.*

hulled steam schooners that had carried most of the lumber cargoes of the Pacific Coast since the 1880s. The old steam schooners and the sailing craft they themselves replaced, had reached the end of their useful lifetime. At the same time, lumber mills had begun to ship timber by road directly to large ports such as Humboldt Bay, making the operation of larger steel-hulled freighters economically feasible, and bypassing the little "doghole" ports along the coast that had made the operation of smaller craft worthwhile.

Vulcan steamed to Norfolk, Virginia where it was altered, modernized, and reconditioned. Emerging as *Coos Bay*, with an enlarged freight capacity, the ship immediately headed for Pacific waters via the Panama Canal, where it began to ply the coastal route, carrying lumber from the seaports of the great Northwest to San Francisco and San Pedro. *Coos Bay* left San Francisco in ballast for Coos Bay, Oregon on October 22, 1927 under the command of Captain B.W. Olson. Departing late in the evening, the ship hit thick fog passing through the Golden Gate. Fog signals echoed condusingly in the close night air. Unknown to those on the bridge, a strong ebb tide and a northwesterly swell caused the ship to stray far out of the main ship channel. The command that swung *Coos Bay*'s bow toward the south was therefore a fatal one, because it had not yet cleared the bight outside the Gate. At 8:06 p.m. the ship struck hard on the rocks at Land's End east of China Beach. The hull tore open and water poured into the engine room. Firemen and engineers fled as the main steam line ruptured, spreading scalding steam into the machinery spaces. The ship lost all power.

The thirty-three-man crew waited out an uncomfortable night on deck as heavy swells battered the vessel. At daybreak rescuers appeared on the scene. The crew readied a breeches buoy and fired the Lyle gun up over the looming cliffs. That first shot had too great a charge, and sailed over the heads of the assembled crowd, to crash into the home of a very surprised E.A. Kinney at 3633 Clement Street. Subsequent shots found their mark, however, and fourteen crew members were hauled ashore over the surf by rescue line. The rest were removed by boat.

Within twenty-four hours *Coos Bay*'s decks had split under the tremendous pounding of the seas. All further efforts to free the ship failed. Abandoned, the freighter changed into a twisted hulk. For several years, the wreck remained relatively intact, and was a source of amusement for curiosity-seekers. The bow became bent and wrenched free, but much of the hull remained above water. Some members of the civic community were not amused, and complained "over the appearance of the stranded craft at the entrance to the bay . . . *Coos Bay*, together with the broken hull of tanker *Lyman Stewart*, which lies nearby, imparts an uninviting appearance to the harbor." The San Francisco Junior Chamber of Commerce promoted a campaign that led to the scrapping of the vessel in April 1930. All that remains visible today is an assortment of battered metal exposed at low tide.

Frank H. Buck
March 6, 1937

Frank H. Buck was launched in 1914 at San Francisco's Union Iron Works. Built for the Associated Oil Company of California, the ship was named for its

Scrapped remains of Coos Bay, *April 1930.*

vice-president and director Frank H. Buck of Vacaville. Under a headline "Named for Local Man," the *Vacaville Reporter* noted proudly that, "The boat is the largest oil tank steamer flying the American flag, having 18 oil tanks and a carrying capacity of 62,000 barrels of oil. The length is 410 feet and it will cost approximately a million dollars when completed." Designed to carry bulk cargoes for California's rapidly growing petroleum industry, tankers like *Buck* and its ill-fated sister ship *Lyman A. Stewart* came into their own on the West Coast after spectacular discoveries of new oil fields in the last decade of the nineteenth century caused "a revolutionary transformation of the economies of southern California and the coast." Large oil refineries sprang up on the shores of San Francisco Bay as well as in the Southland, while the use of the automobile grew explosively, and forever changed the course of California's history.

Frank H. Buck had an adventurous career that first took her between New York and far-flung ports in Europe, Central America, and Asia. When the First World War broke out, the Navy requisitioned the tanker for service as an oiler, arming it with a 6-inch and a 4-inch gun for defensive purposes. *Buck* got to use them. In July 1918 the tanker exchanged fire with a German U-boat outside New York Harbor, but escaped unscathed. On September 13, 1918, it was credited with the remarkable feat of sinking another surfaced U-boat that opened fire on the tanker in mid-Atlantic.

Returned to its original owners in January 1919, *Buck* continued its adventures and brushes with disaster. One time the rudder was wrenched free by heavy seas but the ship made port at Eureka, California under a jury-rigged rudder. In 1924 the tanker ran aground at Point Pinos near Monterey because of a navigational error. The owners had *Buck*, holed and leaking, patched, towed free, and repaired. In 1935, bullets fired from a high-powered rifle struck the ship as it crossed the Carquinez Straits at a time when tankships were involved in a labor dispute. *Frank H. Buck* survived its sister ship *Lyman Stewart* by fifteen years, but met a similar end at the same spot, in what is surely the greatest coincidence in the annals of shipwrecks at the Golden Gate.

On March 6, 1937, bound through the Golden Gate for Martinez with a full cargo of oil from Ventura, *Frank H. Buck* was rammed head-on by the Dollar Lines luxury passenger liner *President Coolidge*, outward bound for the Orient. Although conditions were generally clear inside the bay, the fog dropped like a curtain just at the Golden Gate Bridge. *Coolidge* and *Buck* heard warning signals too late, and took evasive action only when collision was unavoidable.

At the nearby Marine Exchange station at Land's End, the lookout "heard the fog horns of both vessels for some minutes before the crash." "The fog was too thick to see anything. . . ." he said, "then, all of a sudden came the crash. Through the heavy fog it sounded like a big, muffled boom of a Presidio gun. At once the *Coolidge* . . . sent up three short whistle blasts and I knew right away something went wrong, for that was a distress signal. After that there was an awful silence, broken only by buoy horns."

Although sizeable, *Buck* was no match for *President Coolidge*, at thirty-two thousand tons one of the two largest passenger vessels under the American flag. Although its bow was crushed, *Coolidge* was not in any danger of sinking. The luxury liner's rail was soon "lined with attractive society girls and teachers

bound for world cruises." The lovely ladies, diplomats, honeymooners, and businessmen were enthralled witnesses to the rescue of the stricken tanker's crew. Under Capt. R.W. Kelly, *Buck* headed away from the cliffs of the northern headlands, in hopes that the strong ebb would carry the vessel to where it could be beached. When the vessel was down by the bow and trailing oil, the crew was ordered into the lifeboats. Quick and efficient lowering of the boats, and the prompt response by rescue craft from the Coast Guard and the San Francisco Police Department, were largely responsible for saving all hands. The single casualty of the collision was a minor head wound incurred as a crewman leapt into the lifeboat. Even the ship's dog was saved.

Captain K.A. Ahlin of *President Coolidge* contributed to the successful rescue by coolly keeping the great liner's bow wedged as long as possible into the hole in *Buck*'s side. He later declared that the accident was "one of those things that are over before you can see them . . . Our engines were full astern at the time we hit. We could not see the tanker until she was almost on us." Gushing oil, the mortally wounded tanker drifted on the ebb tide until it came to rest, bow in the sand and rocks, and stern out of water, across the bay directly off Land's End. The tanker ended up within shouting distance of the remains of its sister ship, *Lyman Stewart*.

Although the stern continued for some time to swing free in the currents of the ship channel, *Buck*'s bow remained wedged firmly in the rocks, and all attempts to free the vessel failed. Some sixty thousand gallons of oil — most of the cargo — was pumped into barges alongside, avoiding a disastrous oil spill. The remains were dynamited in 1938 to clear the harbor approach of the numerous and obvious shipwreck hulks. Years later, the engine and sternpost can still be seen at low water, next to the engine of the *Lyman Stewart*.

Boiler fires still burning in the unflooded after spaces, the tanker Frank H. Buck *comes to rest at lands End after a collision with the liner* President Coolidge *on March 6, 1937.*

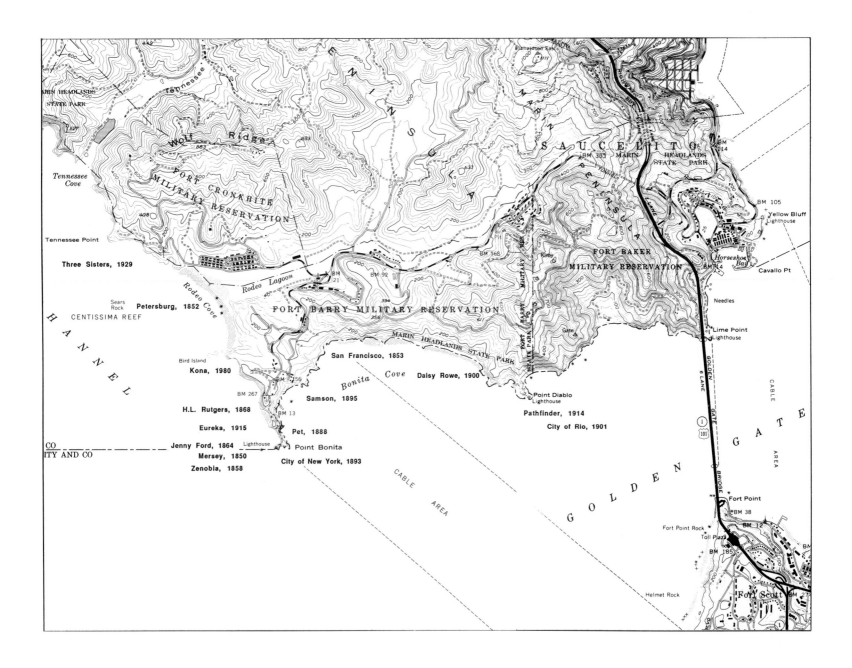

Chapter 4
Shipwrecks On The Marin Coast

The north shore of the Golden Gate was a heavily used area of vessel traffic. Swift currents and other hazards combined with the large volume of shipping to litter its shores with shipwrecks. High on the list of dangers are the fierce currents that sweep in and out of the narrow entrance to wide San Francisco Bay. As the tide changes, or as the flowing water is deflected by the several points of land that jut into the channel, confusing and dangerous back eddies are formed. The high cliffs that line the Marin County shore are unforgiving to grounded vessels. Point Bonita, Point Diablo, and Lime Point protrude into the water. Deep water close to shore makes casting the lead an insufficient warning method. Thick fogs blanket the area both summer and winter. Sailing craft close to the cliffs are somewhat in the wind shadow from the prevailing north-westerlies, but vessels are given no lee at all from the more dangerous southerly winds that accompany winter storms.

Running south from the sands of Stinson Beach to Point Bonita is a stretch of coastline consisting largely of high cliffs falling steeply to a rocky shore. The jagged coast and offshore rocks are interrupted for only three beaches of significant size — Rodeo, Tennessee, and Muir. Fog often shrouds the coastline, and soundings show deep water up to a few score yards of the shore. As elsewhere, the prevailing northwest winds blow onshore. It is perhaps because Duxbury Reef, and farther north Point Reyes, jut out so far from the general line of the coast that more wrecks have not occurred along this portion of the coast. Nevertheless, the wrecks described in this chapter include the historically significant and exciting.

Mersey
December 16, 1850

Mersey was a three-masted bark built at Montreal in

1840, owned by Buchanan of Liverpool, and used in trans-Atlantic service between the dominion of Canada and the mother country of Great Britain. Damaged in 1848, *Mersey* nevertheless was able to rate a very high classification from Lloyds' surveyors. The bark evidently came to California as one of the multitude of vessels carrying argonauts bound for the gold fields, but went ashore on December 16, 1850 at a small point of land halfway between Point Bonita and Point Diablo.

The story of the wreck is a mystery. What is known comes from a letter the master, William Cobbin, published in the San Francisco press, stating that the cargo had been consigned to Messrs. Starkey Brothers & Co., and that a certain amount of money was on board. He named "bad weather" the culprit. All hands were saved "with the greatest difficulty," but "the ship is a total wreck." Afterwards it was boarded at low water, and a mate attempted to recover some of the crew's effects with the aid of a launch from the *U.S.S. Savannah*.

Tagus
August 3, 1851

As the markets based on the California gold rush market boomed in late 1850 and early 1851, many vessels sailed for San Francisco carrying greater quantities of cargo and fewer passengers. One such vessel was the ship *Tagus* of Boston. On February 8, 1851, *Tagus* sailed from New York for San Francisco. After a 179-day passage, *Tagus* lay off the Golden Gate in a thick fog on August 2, 1851, in the company of the

Australian vessel *Mary Catherine*. Both vessels took on pilots, and *Mary Catherine* anchored while *Tagus* continued on. The next day *Mary Catherine* safely passed through the harbor entrance on August 3, when its passengers and crew learned that *Tagus* had missed the Golden Gate in the fog and had run ashore four miles north of the Gate.

On August 4 the steamer *California* sailed to the wreck to haul it off, but could not do so. *Tagus* was declared a total loss but "most of the cargo will probably be saved. . . . Several schooners and lighters are engaged in getting out her cargo." By August 8 most of the cargo had been landed in San Francisco. "Consignees by the ship *Tagus* are informed that a considerable portion of the cargo has been landed here by the Salvors, which is ready for delivery upon securing the freight, salvage charges, and expenses. The balance of the cargo not yet at hand, will be saved, and will be delivered as it arrives." Ultimately all of the cargo was salvaged, but *Tagus* stayed on the beach of small "Potato Cove," renamed Tennessee Cove two years later when the steamer *Tennessee* was lost at the same spot.

Petersburg
August 23, 1852

Built at New York in 1837, the 183-ton brig *Petersburg* was engaged in coastal trade, joining three separate packet lines in her East Coast career. In 1843 *Petersburg* traded between New York and Veracruz, Mexico. In 1848 the brig sailed for the "Union Line" between New York and Savannah, and in 1849 for the "Merchant's

Line" between New York and Charleston. Registered at New York, *Petersburg* hailed from that port through 1850, sailing for California late in the year. Sold to Capt. W.H. Pike of San Francisco in March 1851, *Petersburg* was one of many small sailing craft that traded between various ports of call and the gold rush city. A detailed accounting of *Petersburg*'s short California career is unavailable, but it is recorded that the brig called at Sacramento in 1851. An indication of its cargoes can be found in an advertisement in the San Francisco *Daily Alta California* of August 8, 1851. "POTATOES—The cargo of the brig *Petersburg*, from Sandwich Islands, in prime order, for sale by GANO & GRIDLEY, Pacific Wharf, cor. Battery st." *Petersburg* was owned and commanded by Capt. Pike of San Francisco. On Monday, August 23, 1852 *Petersburg* went ashore in fog, wrecking a mile north of Point Bonita in Rodeo Cove, "close to where the *Tagus* was wrecked. . . ." *Petersburg* carried a cargo of general produce, "which may be saved, though it is thought that the vessel will be a total loss." No other mention of the wreck of *Petersburg* was made.

Tennessee
March 6, 1853

The 1,275-ton wooden side-wheel steamship *Tennessee* was built by William H. Webb at New York in 1848. Launched on October 25, 1848, *Tennessee* was fitted with a single side-lever steam engine. The steamer was built for the New York and Savannah Steam Navigation Company of New York, which operated *Tennessee* and its sister ship *Cherokee* in a bimonthly steam line between Savannah and New York. The steamers carried passengers, high freight goods, and cotton. A substantial area of the South was served by the New York and Savannah Steam Navigation Company; in 1848 it was noted "this line is now patronized by New Orleans travellers, and also those going to Florida, Alabama and Tennessee, with which places the railroad communication from Savannah is now nearly complete."

Tennessee withdrew from the New York and Savannah run in October 1849 after its fifteenth voyage, following the steamer's sale to Howland and Aspinwall of New York for $200,000. The new owners modified *Tennessee* to carry more passengers, and in December 1849 sent the ship into the Pacific to join the Pacific Mail Steamship Company's line of steamers connecting Panama and San Francisco. The California gold rush had attracted tens of thousands of eager fortune-seekers to the Panama route, and dozens of vessels, sail and steam, busily served as the oceanic links of the route. *Tennessee*, in joining the Pacific Mail fleet, became the first of many American steamships to be disrupted in their regular routes and pressed into service on the Pacific for the gold rush.

Arriving on the Pacific Coast in the spring of 1850, *Tennessee* served as an important link of empire, aiding to establish regular service between the Atlantic seaboard and Europe and the new territory of California with steamships on both sides of the continent. In its cabins and staterooms, *Tennessee* carried those who wished to make their fortunes in California at the "gold diggings" and those who had either made their "pile" or went home "bust." The ship transported luxury items, valuable freight, and

The March 1853 wreck of the Pacific Mail *steamer* Tennessee *gave Tennessee Cove a name.*

California's mineral wealth. *Tennessee* was also a link to the more familiar world that the gold-seekers, who fancied themselves the "argonauts of '49," left behind. The printed word and the mail were among the most eagerly anticipated items *Tennessee* and its running mates carried to and from California. *Tennessee* served on the Panama route for nearly three years, making twenty-nine voyages between Panama and San Francisco with passengers, high-duty freight, mail, and specie until lost on March 6, 1853 three miles north of Point Bonita.

On that foggy morning, *Tennessee* lay at anchor near the Farallone Islands, twenty-six miles west of the Golden Gate. Although visibility was limited to sixty feet, Capt. Edward Mellus was confident of his position, and commenced to navigate the steamer slowly ahead, occasionally stopping to take soundings with the lead. He was unaware of the outgoing tide's strong current that swept *Tennessee* north past the Gate and along the Marin shore. Soon a rock loomed out of the fog, and Mellus, supposing it to be Mile Rock, ordered more steam to be made. At 9 a.m., while standing on the open bridge atop one of the steamer's paddlewheel boxes, he heard breakers ahead. Simultaneously the lookout at the bow sighted breakers, and Capt. Mellus ordered the engines reversed. Rocks blocked *Tennessee*, however, and the ship began to swing broadside towards the rock-bound shoreline. The fog lifted enough for Mellus to see a narrow opening in the cliffs and a small sandy beach. To avoid the considerable loss of life that could be expected if *Tennessee* struck the rocks, Mellus took the hard but unavoidable choice of beaching the ship on the sands of Tennessee Cove. Broadsided and hard ashore, the steamer heeled sharply to port. "It seemed

a great shudder went through the ship, and the hull, and the masts, and the engines, and all things that were on her trembled."

Passengers screamed and ran up on deck. One later recalled "there came an awful crash of the steamer. . . Everything went off the table in a heap. . . ." In the midst of great confusion, a few of the passengers and crew sprang into purposeful action, managing to secure a hawser to the rocks ashore to guide the ship's boats to safety. All women and children were landed first, followed by the male passengers and crew, mail and baggage. The unruly and panicked were held back at pistol point. The passengers built fires along the beach from the wreckage to keep warm and dry while help was summoned, and set up tents for shelter that night.

The next morning help arrived in the form of the United States Ship *Warren*, the steamer *Confidence*, and the tug *Goliah*. It was hoped that *Tennessee* could be pulled off. "She is perfectly tight, and although her copper is much chafed and rubbed off, there is every reason to suppose that no serious injury has thus far been sustained." However, heavy surf on March 8 broke *Tennessee*'s back, ruptured the steam pipes, and split the hull, flooding the ship. A visit to the wreck on March 10:

revealed her condition to be perfectly hopeless, and her situation almost unfavorable for the preservation of the valuable portions of her machinery and fixtures. She is fast going to pieces. Every joist appeared started. The sea was thumping heavily against her side, and the surf flying wildly over her. She cannot hold together another week.

The crew had already salvaged the gold, mail, and baggage; salvors stripped the steamer of furniture and equipment through March 19. By that time, the stack had fallen, the deck had collapsed, and the starboard side was breached in several places. By March 21 *Tennessee* disintegrated into the surf, leaving its name to mark the wreck site at "Tennessee Cove."

San Francisco

December 8, 1853

San Francisco was a graceful extreme clipper — a classic example of the famous type built for the California trade. Built in New York for local merchants Rich & Elam and Thomas Wardle, *San Francisco* was commanded by Capt. Tetzer. On its one and only voyage, the clipper carried passengers and general cargo consigned to Rich and Elam. Clearing New York on October 25, 1853, *San Francisco* passed Cape Horn without incident, and was becalmed for three days 450 miles from the Golden Gate. The ship then groped its way through four days of fog that lifted a half-mile off the Farallon Islands.

San Francisco picked up a pilot off the Farallones, and sailed under his direction into San Francisco Bay. As the ship passed close by Point Bonita, it was caught in an eddy and missed stays coming about. Swirling about, *San Francisco* hit the rocks near the Point, and lost jibbom, bowsprit, head, and cutwater. Drifting clear, the badly damaged clipper anchored in Bonita Cove with seawater rising in the hold. The steam tugs *Abby Holmes* and *Resolute* came

to its aid, removing passengers, and attempting to pump out the water that filled the vessel. But the damage was too great. San Francisco shipped anchor and was towed "close inshore," where the ship filled and came to rest in the cove on its port beam with the starboard waterways awash. The sea was calm, and hope was held that "if the weather continues fine, most of the cargo will be saved in a damaged condition . . . the vessel will probably become a total loss, and a bad loss it is."

The notorious Capt. Robert H. "Bully" Waterman, former master of the reputed "hell ship" *Challenge*, bought the wreck and cargo for $12,000, in partnership with a Capt. Wright. The clipper was valued at $103,000 to $125,000 and cargo at $150,000 to $400,000, so there seemed to be a good chance of a killing to be made on the investment. However, a veritable "multitude of plunderers hastened to the wreck and proceeded to help themselves, owner's and agent's representatives vainly attempting to drive them away. Many were armed and defied opposition, fought among themselves, and frequently stole each other's booty. It was reported that soldiers from the Presidio, across the Golden Gate, were among the crowd."

On December 9 a storm came up that wreaked havoc among the looters. "Several boats were stove alongside or destroyed attempting to land in the surf." The half-decked sloop *Midnight City*, belonging to Capt. Hill, who owned one of the numerous storeships grounded at Yerba Buena Cove, drifted out to sea and was lost with its drunken crew of eight. A whitehall boat with two looters was swamped and the men drowned. "Lighters, tugboats and steamers" scattered for their lives, many seeking shelter in Horseshoe and Richardson's bays, while "a large number of packages of goods were found floating in the bay. . . ."

The beautiful clipper *San Francisco* soon degenerated into "a complete and perfect wreck. Her foremast has gone by the board, and in falling it carried away the main yard. . . . The sails and part of the running rigging, as well as a portion of her cargo, were taken out. . . . Her upper deck is cut open fore and aft as far as could be to enable the persons employed to remove the cargo. Hundreds of boats are on the ground saving what they can."

Zenobia
April 30, 1858

The 630-ton ship *Zenobia* was built at Medford, Massachusetts in 1838. In 1853 *Zenobia* was a packet sailing between Philadelphia and Liverpool. Sometime after 1854 the ship sailed into the Pacific, where *Zenobia* was lost near the Point Bonita lighthouse in 1858 with a precious freight. The ship had been returning from Sitka, Alaska with a cargo of ice from the American Russian Ice Company worth $30,000. The ice trade was one aspect of coastal trade that boomed as a result of the California gold rush and the rise of San Francisco. Russian visitors to San Francisco during the gold rush noted the need for ice, then brought by an occasional sawdust-packed cargo around Cape Horn from New England, which also supplied the Mediterranean, South America, and the southern United States. Ice from Alaska would come faster, though, and in 1852 the first ice cargo from the

Russian Ice Company of Sitka arrived aboard the bark *Backus*. In just sixteen days, a much desired "luxury in San Francisco" was delivered to the city's doorstep. Just one week after *Backus'* arrival on April 11, wagons from the consignee, The Pacific Ice Co., were distributing the frozen product throughout the city.

Zenobia was one of the many ships that followed *Backus*. Owned by the American Russian Commerical Company of San Francisco, the ship was under the command of Capt. J.B. Tilden. As he approached the Golden Gate, Tilden refused assistance from the pilot boats *Golden Gate* and *Daniel Webster*, standing by. But when the tide turned and the wind died, *Zenobia* was caught in a strong back eddy and swept "upon the outer rock which forms the extreme point of the North Head." Lighthouse keeper Chapman and whitehall boatman Frank Murphy were able to save "part of the clothing of the crew," while the men "were saved by means of a whaleboat belonging to the ship, which, as the wind increased, was the only class of boat which could get near her."

As *Zenobia* disintegrated, "the bottom came up to the surface . . . and floated in pieces into the harbor. The masts were standing at sundown, but doubtless went by the board during the night. Small portions of the rigging, and some of the sails in a damaged condition, may be saved." Poor return indeed for the vessel and its cargo — and classic proof of the wisdom of employing bar pilots at the hazardous bay entrance.

The battered wreckage of the ship Elizabeth at Slide Ranch, described by contemporary newspaper reports as "scattered, mashed, and pulverized...a breakwater of matchwood a third of a mile long." Eighteen men, including the captain, died in the wreck on February 21, 1891.

Jenny Ford
February 1, 1864

Jenny Ford was a Maine-built, 397-ton barkentine that came West in the wake of the gold rush. Built at East Machias in 1854 specifically for the Pacific Coast lumber trade, *Jenny Ford* was registered in San Francisco under the house flag of the pioneer lumber firm of Pope and Talbot. Throughout its career *Jenny Ford* sailed between San Francisco and the early lumber ports of the northwest; a year before its loss the barkentine arrived at San Francisco from Puget Sound with twenty thousand pilings. *Jenny Ford* was lost on the rocks near the lighthouse at Point Bonita on February 1, 1864, when it missed stays trying to come about in the north channel. Two men drowned as the vessel hit the shore broadside and lost fifteen feet of the bow. Scavengers had a field day, helping themselves to the sails and rigging. Although it was said that the vessel's starboard side was gone as far aft as the mizzen and only the mizzenmast still stood, the steam tug *Merrimac* was able to pull the hulk free and tow it to Rincon Point in San Francisco Bay. The remains were sold at auction several days later for a mere $310, although wags speculated that the purchaser could only obtain firewood from the remains.

H.L. Rutgers
January 1, 1868

The bark *H.L. Rutgers* was a typical bluff-bowed cargo carrier, built on pre-clipper lines at Perth Amboy, New Jersey in 1855. Owned first by Laban Howes, and then by the Western Union Telegraph Company, the bark joined the Russian American Telegraph Construction Fleet. At the time of loss the ship was partly owned by Adams, Blinn & Co., who employed it in the lumber trade. The other portion of *Rutgers* had been owned by an unnamed Confederate officer whose interest was confiscated during the Civil War.

On January 1, 1868 the newspapers reported that *H.L. Rutgers*, inbound from Seabeck (Washington Territory) with a cargo of piles and sawn lumber, had gotten into difficulty in the Potato Patch, and was lying "just outside the North Head, and exhibited signals of distress." One boat had been carried away, and "seas were breaking over her badly at times." Capt. Marston, penny-wise and pound-foolish, refused the aid of the tugs *Rescue* and *Lookout*, believing he could ride out the rough weather. On the morning of New Year's Day, the bark had worked in so far toward the rocky shore that a great sea disabled the rudder. The captain then had no choice but to accept aid.

The two tugs returned and tried twice to pull *H.L. Rutgers* off, but were twice foiled when the towing hawsers parted. A party of men who had crossed to the Marin shore were able to get the crew ashore by making a line fast between the vessel and the beach, but *Rutgers* had gone "broadside on the rocks in a little cove or bay just beyond the Light House, on the north side of Point Bonita," so near shore that the crew might have escaped by climbing ashore on the fallen masts if they had not come down on the wrong side of the vessel. The bottom "was soon pounded out of the *Rutgers* and her masts falling through the breach, [she] soon began to break up. . . and next morning only a confused mass of broken timbers and loose lumber floating in the surf marked the place of the wreck."

William Mighel
February 12, 1873

The small twenty-five-ton schooner *William Mighel* ran between Point Reyes and San Francisco carrying produce and dairy goods. Bound for Tomales, the schooner was run down and sunk off Point Bonita by the steamer *Prince Alfred* on February 12, 1873. One of *Mighel*'s crew was killed.

Patrician
February 28, 1873

The British ship *Patrician* was built of teak at Sunderland in 1859 for George Marshall and Son. The ship ranged far, serving in the Cape Horn and Australian trades. Under the command of Capt. F.J. Wilson, the ship arrived at San Francisco from Hong Kong early in 1873. Lying off San Francisco for five weeks, *Patrician* loaded grain. Clearing San Francisco on the morning of February 28 for Cork, Ireland, the ship was towed past the Golden Gate by the tug *Wizard* in company with the clipper *Young America* and the bark *La Escocesa*. Crowds turned out on the waterfront to watch the three ships depart.

At 4:30 p.m., just as pilot William H. Diggo left the ship, *Patrician* struck a submerged obstruction off Point Bonita with a crash that shook the hull "from deck to keelson." The bottom was stove in, and within minutes seven feet of water filled the hold. The pumps were overwhelmed. The thirty-one-man crew was rescued by tugs as the ship ran aground in sixteen feet of water in the midst of Potato Patch Shoal. Though never proved, waterfront speculators claimed *Patrician* had run over the wreck of *William Mighel*, lost at the same spot two weeks earlier.

Prince Alfred
June 14, 1874

The 815-ton, iron-hulled steamship *Prince Alfred* was built at Sunderland, Great Britain in 1852. The steamer's engines were display pieces from the Great Exhibition at London's Crystal Palace in 1851. *Prince Alfred* first arrived at San Francisco on June 6, 1870 "from Central American ports," and soon thereafter was sold to entrepreneurs who fitted it up to work between San Francisco and Victoria, British Columbia. For the remainder of its career *Prince Alfred* remained on the Victoria run, carrying passengers, cargo, and the mails. An old vessel at the time of loss, a contract had already been signed to replace the engines.

Prince Alfred departed Victoria on June 11, 1874 with eighty-five passengers and a cargo of "100 bags of charcoal, 1 package of castings, three cases gaiters, 21 bundles of deer skins, 3 cases effects, 1 organ, 2 bundles and 213 hides, 31 sacks of furs, 75 bags of coal, 37 bales of wood, 3 packages merchandise and $24,127 in treasure."

On June 14, 1874 in a thick coastal fog, *Prince Alfred* struck lightly on Duxbury Reef. The impact was

An excursion streamer visits the wreck of S.S. City of New York *soon after the* Pacific Mail *steamship's October 26, 1893 stranding at Point Bonita.*

so slight that the vessel continued on until the chief engineer informed the captain that water was pouring into the ship from a ten-foot-square hole punched through the side. The crew extinguished the boilers to keep them from exploding if cold seawater hit the hot metal, and raised sail in an attempt to run for shore. *Prince Alfred* ran aground on the rocks at Potato Cove, just north of Tennessee Cove. "During all the affair the passengers and crew behaved with great coolness, which is remarkable, considering many ladies were among the passengers." All aboard safely landed, the crew bringing the treasure and mail to San Francisco in a boat. Three tugs were dispatched to the wreck, but *Prince Alfred* sank and could not be salvaged. Some of the cargo washed ashore after the wreck, but the remainder stayed on the bottom with the steamer.

Rescue
October 3, 1874

Rescue was a powerful steam-screw tugboat, owned by one of San Francisco's premier tugboat operators, Capt. Griffith & Co. Built in 1865, the iron-hulled, 139-ton tugboat was involved in several ship rescues in the course of its brief nine-year career, including unsuccessful attempts to save the ship *Viscata* and the bark *H.L. Rutgers* in 1868. While returning to San Francisco after towing the bark *Cleta* to sea, *Rescue* ran shore and wrecked at Point Bonita. Running "full steam" in spite of dense fog at the Point, the tug struck "just under the lighthouse . . . with a tremendous shock" at 11 o'clock on the night of October 3, 1874. The one casualty was a young lad named Thomas

Markey who had just come along "for the ride." He was tossed overboard by the impact and lost. Boatman Steve Castle, defying great danger, went out in his boat and took the crew off the wreck. By the next evening *Rescue*, "beyond rescue," sank at the Point and became an uninsured total loss.

Pet
September 1888

The two-masted schooner *Pet* was a forty-nine-ton vessel built in 1868 at Fisherman's Bay, California. Registered at San Francisco, *Pet* was one of hundreds of two-masted schooners on the coast. These tiny, hard-working craft went about their careers in anonymity, and *Pet* is known to history only because of her loss. The story quoted below appeared in the *Los Angeles Times* on September 20, 1888.

> *Word was received at the [San Francisco] Merchant's Exchange today that the schooner Pet of this port [San Francisco] had gone ashore at North Heads. . . . shortly afterward, the schooner Sarah Alexander, Capt. Cousens, which left here this morning for Salt Point, returned to port, having on board the captain's wife and three of the men composing the crew of the schooner Pet, and having the Pet's boat in tow. One of the men, Henry Wauhermann, had been injured severely when the vessel struck the rocks, and was suffering greatly. On landing, the captain's wife and crew stated that the schooner left here for Albion river on*

Saturday noon, and during the evening, when outside, fell calm and she began to drift. Fearing that if the wind did not spring up that the vessel would be dashed on the rocks, Capt. Purcher ordered the crew into boats with his wife and he, himself, stuck by the vessel hoping if wind sprang up that he might be able to save her which he could do as well without as with the crew. The boat stayed by the schooner awhile and then pulled out to sea and [was] picked up by the schooner Sarah Alexander, which was sailing out of the harbor, as stated, and brought it to Meiggs' wharf. It was learned to-night that the captain is safe.

Elizabeth

February 21, 1891

The downeaster *Elizabeth* was a 1,866-ton wooden ship built at Newcastle, Maine and launched in 1882, and owned largely by Searsport, Maine sea captains, "active and retired, and their relatives." On its maiden voyage *Elizabeth* sailed to Japan, Seattle, San Francisco, Liverpool, and New York. Thereafter all the ship's voyages were from New York to San Francisco, returning by way of England. *Elizabeth* carried general cargoes to San Francisco, there loading with California grain for Liverpool. In all, *Elizabeth* made six round-trip voyages and was lost on the seventh.

Arriving off the Golden Gate on February 21, 1891, *Elizabeth* brought a varied cargo of iron rails, pipe, ink, whiskey, burlap, and other general merchandise consigned to Williams, Dimond &

Company. Despite rapidly deteriorating weather conditions, Capt. J. Herbert Colcord thought he could work his ship through the Gate, and refused the offer of a tow from the tug *Monarch* in order to save $50. Colcord was a famous New England seagoing family name, and the captain apparently had more than his share of pride and confidence in his skill. He got as far into the harbor as Lime Point before the wind shifted and combined with "the strong eddy, and the heave of the sea" to drive *Elizabeth* back toward Point Bonita. The tugs *Alert* and *Reliance* were hailed just before the ship went onto the rocks, but more dickering over the price of a tow delayed the taking of a line aboard, even as "the ship was fast driving towards the shore." When the towing hawser parted, *Elizabeth* began to drive past Point Bonita, swept out by the ebb tide and southeast wind, yards aback, in spite of the best efforts of *Alert*. The ship grounded on Four Fathom Bank in the Potato Patch. With heavy seas breaking over the decks, the vessel began to fill with water.

Captain Colcord and his son were swept off the poop onto the main deck. The tugs again approached and took off Capt. Colcord's wife and family as *Elizabeth* drifted off the bank and continued north, while the wounded master stayed aboard with the rest of the crew. Both tugs had to flee for their lives as heavy seas opened up hull plates and sea water rose in the engine rooms to near the level of the boiler fires. Capt. John Silovich of the tug *Alert* later remembered, "It was blowing a hurricane, the sea was sharp and choppy, and little headway could be made. With hawsers breaking, lifeboats tossing and seas flooding every deck, it was a scene never to be forgotten. No boat could have survived beyond the heads. Just at this time an enormous sea threw one of the lifeboats

The pilotboat Pathfinder, *a total loss at Point Diablo on January 15, 1914.*

partly under and athwart the bow of the tug, and the keeper shouted, 'Cut the tow line!'" Without immediate assistance, *Elizabeth* was doomed. Striking again at Tennessee Cove, *Elizabeth* drifted off again, finally going ashore seven miles north of Point Bonita at Big Slide Ranch. Going into the rocks, the ship quickly disintegrated, killing eighteen of the twenty-six-man crew. Among the dead was Capt. Colcord.

Crews from the United States Life-Saving Stations at Golden Gate Park and Fort Point responded to the wreck, but their heroic efforts were doomed to failure. The Fort Point surfboat, in the tow of a tug, was swamped. Keeper Charles Henry washed overboard and drowned. Keeper Hollohan of the Golden Gate Park Station then took some of the Fort Point crew, crossed the bay to Sausalito by ferry, and unable to secure horses from local liveries, "directed his men to harness themselves to the drag ropes of the cart, which, with its load weighted nearly a ton and a half, and started for the scene of the disaster. The road led them over high hills and through deep ravines of adobe mud and soft slippery clay, but the faithful surfmen tugged on until about 5 o'clock in the morning, when they reached a point . . . about eight miles from Sausalito where they halted." Horses were finally secured at Tennessee Ranch, and the party quickly reached the ocean shore at Tennessee Cove. Upon arrival, the exhausted life-savers found that *Elizabeth* had pulled free and drifted farther north. Continuing their trek along the rugged Northern Marin coast, they finally arrived at the wreck, too late to help. The life-savers had responded to the disaster in the best tradition of their service, only to be thwarted by the weather.

The wreck was described as a vessel "ground to splinters":

Scattered, mashed, and pulverized, the ship herself lined the shore—a breakwater of matchwood a third of a mile long . . . . Here and there, on some jagged rock near the bar, a vaster lump of wreckage than any in the pulpy breakwater could be seen. The solid stern, almost flattened by the battering it received, abutted the surf at one point. It had been lifted bodily over a twenty-foot crag and flung on the rock coast about fifteen yards beyond.

The remains lay in large distinct pieces, tossed ashore. The port side of the bow lay in deeper water, however, weighed down by the port bower and the locker chain.

Local residents, after helping save eight crew members who washed ashore, aided in the task of searching through the splinters of wreckage for the badly pounded bodies. Most of the dead were recovered, among the last being the captain, who washed ashore two days after the wreck. The flotsam in the surf was carefully picked over, but little was saved. Four days after *Elizabeth*'s wreck, the cargo salvaged from the beach was sold at auction, bringing only $650, while the wreck sold for $200.

However, the ship "contained a good deal of heavy freight that sank the instant the ship broke in two," and Capt. T.P. Whitelaw was engaged to salvage it. Using the wrecking schooner *Samson* (fated to be driven ashore and lost less than two years later) as a working platform, Whitelaw sent divers down to salvage what they could from "the heterogenous mass of stuff" that had once been *Elizabeth*.

The disaster that befell *Elizabeth* was a great tragedy for the Pacific Coast maritime community. The dramatic strength of the gale that blew the ship to its doom, the heroic rescue of Capt. Colcord's wife and family, the efforts of the life-savers, and the loss of Keeper Henry, as well as the complete destruction of the ship and much of the crew, made the wreck of *Elizabeth* "one of the worst disasters that has happened on the coast for a number of years."

City of New York
October 26, 1893

The decades after the Civil War were a period of neglect for the American merchant marine. In the early 1870s only three yards in the whole country were capable of building modern iron-hulled steamers of large size (more than two thousand tons). One was the Chester, Pennsylvania shipyard of John Roach, where *City of New York* was launched in 1875. Roach, a controversial figure, was a well-known builder of vessels for steamship lines and the United States government. Among his clients was the Pacific Mail Steamship Company, for whom he constructed the largest vessels built or owned in America at the time — the sister steam propeller liners *City of Tokio* and *City of Peking*. Also constructed in his yard were two other vessels that met tragic ends in the waters of the Golden Gate, *City of Chester* and *City of Rio de Janeiro*.

City of New York and its near-sisters were designed and built to make American vessels competitive again in world trade, and to replace the earlier generation of wooden-hulled sidewheel steamers that dated to the gold rush and the first years of Pacific shipping. Pacific Mail, spurred by the success of the transcontinental railroad, began to supplement its Panama-to-California route with trade to Australia and the Orient in the decade after the Civil War. Although first-class facilities were a prominent feature of their vessels, the passenger service to Asiatic ports was rendered profitable by the importing of great numbers of "coolie laborers" into the United States to build railroads, and labor in the mines and other industries of the Pacific Coast states.

Cargo trade consisted of manufactured goods, flour, canned goods, and a variety of other foodstuffs expected to find a market in Asia. These items were sent west in exchange for spices, bamboo, indigo, rice, silk, rubber goods, and the many curios considered "exotic" in the West. For almost two decades *City of New York* made a reputation as a good ship, as it plied the sea routes between San Francisco and China, Panama, and Australia.

On October 26, 1893, *City of New York* stood away from the Pacific Mail dock and headed out through the Golden Gate bound for China, under the direction of pilot George Johnson. "There was the heaviest fog on at the time that had been known in years," the tides were "the highest of the month," and the "light from the tower on Point Bonita was eclipsed entirely and the metal mouth of the warning siren at that place had been so deflected as to throw its volume out seaward and render its weird cry worse than useless to the outgoing craft." Now off course to the north without anyone's knowledge, the vessel struck gently on submerged rocks about one hundred yards offshore, to the southeast of Point Bonita. A large roller picked up the vessel and deposited it on top of the jagged rocks, bursting the bottom plates and flooding the hold with eight feet of water.

Panic gripped some of the passengers, many of whom were Chinese on their way back to their homeland, berthed in steerage deep below the waterline. As soon as the ship struck, rockets and signal cannon were fired to announce the calamity. The cannon were heard at the Point Lobos Marine Exchange Lookout, and the Fort Point Life-Saving Station. All available assistance was speedily dispatched to the stranded vessel, but tugs found the steamer wedged fast on the rocks.

City of New York met with disaster by a hair. So close was she from the cliff on which the light house stands it was possible to look down on the steamer's decks . . . lights of the vessel were reflected in [the] stretch of water between the vessel and point of land. It did not look to be more than 500 feet out to the place where she was lying and it could hardly be more than that distance from the rocks, as those which fringe the North Heads do not reach out more than 300 yards and beyond that is deep water. Indeed the light-house keeper said that if the steamer had passed 50 feet farther out from shore she would have cleared the rocks entirely.

With help on scene and the vessel in no immediate danger of sinking, despite a heavy sea running, the passengers calmed. Because of the nearby rocks, tugs could not approach the stranded ship, so the life-saving crew from the Fort Point Life-Saving Station took all passengers off and transferred them to waiting rescue craft. The crew of the Golden Gate Park Station arrived and assisted their comrades in removing mail and $241,000 in specie, articles of value, and the effects of the crew. The next day four boats were recovered "that had broken loose from her and were drifting out to sea" with some Chinese passengers aboard.

Salvage efforts commenced, removing part of the cargo of flour, shrimp, beans, and other general goods. They vainly tried to tow the ship free. Later in November stormy weather set in, and all the wreckers on board or moored nearby had to abandon the site for their safety. "For months the big wreck [lay] there dismantled and drear like the decaying carcass of some vast black monster of the sea, sinking inch by inch into the surrounding depths" until a great storm in March 1894 shook the hulk free and deposited it in deep water between the rocks and the shoreline. Even then, divers continued to raise scrap iron from the wreck, working from the barge *Samson*, soon to be the next wreck on the Marin coast.

Samson
January 3, 1895

Captain T.P. Whitelaw made his living from the salvage of wrecked vessels and was, in fact, the best-known operator of his time. His largest craft was the wrecking schooner "barge" *Samson*, built in 1890 and constructed heavily with a shallow draft, in order to stand close inshore under all conditions and serve as a stable platform for dismantling. *Samson* carried a small steam engine on board for hoisting, but depended entirely on tugs for mobility.

Whitelaw's schooner was the primary vessel engaged in the salvage and dismantling of the hulk of *City of New York*, and managed to pass the entire winter of 1893-1894 perilously anchored alongside the wreck. On January 3, 1895, a fierce gale sprang up. To allow *Samson* to swing freely at anchor, the stern moorings were cast off. The bow came around into the steadily increasing gale. As the winds continued to pick up, a second anchor was let go, but by mid-morning the vessel had begun to drag anchor.

Now *Samson* and the men on board were in deadly peril. Flags and blankets were broken out and run up the signal halliards as distress signals. The donkey engine was stoked up, and the whistle blown for help. But sight and sound were drowned out by the howling storm. A boat was launched and sent to the nearby lighthouse wharf to ask that the fog signal be blown to summon aid. Yet even the loud horn was drowned out by the storm, which had grown to "almost unprecedented ferocity." Most of that night the crew of *Samson* burned torchlights to summon aid, but failed to follow the example of the earlier boat and abandon their vessel while there was still time.

Early in the morning the light was spotted by a surfman from the Fort Point Life-Saving Station, and the station-keeper summoned the aid of the tug *Reliance*. With lifeboat and crew from the station in tow, *Reliance* did its best to steam to the rescue, but "the storm was found to be so severe that prudence forbade the continuance of the journey" until daylight. Before dawn, *Samson*'s crew finally decided to abandon ship. A small yawl was put overboard, but broke free after only two men had boarded it. Drifting rapidly to leeward, boat and men disappeared and were never seen again. Eight men crammed into the last boat left and pulled with all their might. They were barely able to make headway, just managing to keep off the shore and avoid being dashed to pieces on the rocks.

In the pre-dawn darkness and the height of the gale's fury, *Samson* went ashore in Bonita Cove. The watchman was cast into the surf and drowned. The three others still on board, including Captain Hamson, struggled ashore with the aid of the lighthouse crew. As daylight came, *Reliance* and the Fort Point life-saving crew appeared on the violent scene, and at great peril took on board *Samson*'s boat with its eight survivors. Later investigation concluded that there was "some misgiving" if enough anchor cable had initially been played out to stabilize the vessel. It was also felt that "if the crew had remained on board instead of taking to their boats the lives of the two divers swept away in the yawl need not have been lost." The hulk of *Samson* caught fire shortly after the storm and was "almost entirely consumed," leaving little trace of the tragic incident.

Daisy Rowe
November 20, 1900

Daisy Rowe was the name of a schooner owned by E. Higgins of Higgins & Collins of San Francisco, employed in the coastal lumber trade between San Francisco and the lumber ports of the Northwest Coast.

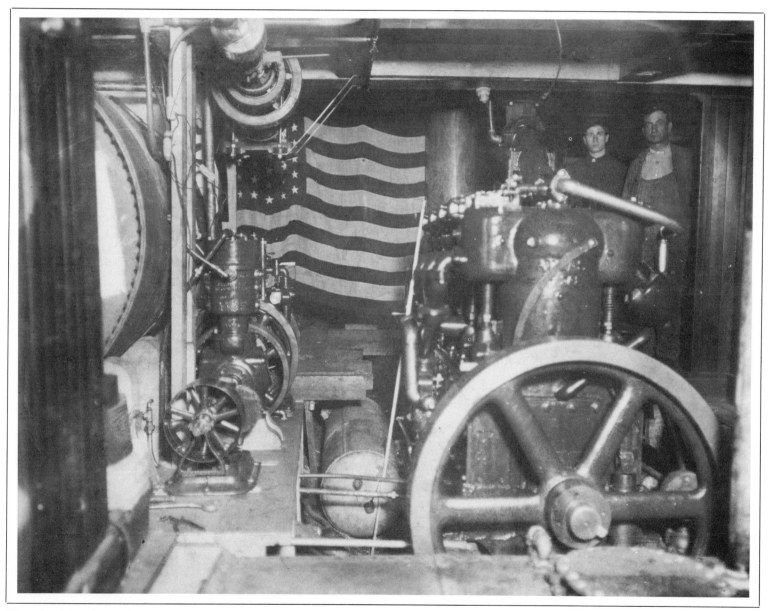

The remains of the auxiliary gasoline engines of the Pathfinder *mark the pilotboat's wreck in the waters off Point Diablo.*

Hans Bendixsen built the schooner in 1879 at Fairhaven (Humboldt Bay), California. *Daisy Rowe* came close to disaster when it lost the foresail and mainmast in a heavy blow at sea on Septmeber 30, 1900 while bound from San Francisco to Grays Harbor, Washington. The steamer *San Blas* spotted *Daisy Rowe* off Point Sur on September 30, but the schooner declined assistance that day and later on the 1st of October, when the steamer *Corona* sighted it. *Daisy Rowe* made Grays Harbor, yet while anchored outside the anchor carried away, and the hardy little schooner was finally forced to hail a tug for assistance to enter the port. Perhaps this voyage was a premonition of things to come, for the next voyage was the last.

Little is known of the wreck event, but the records of the Marine Exchange of San Francisco indicate that *Daisy Rowe* went ashore at 7 p.m. on November 20, "one mile inside Point Bonita," a location just west of Point Diablo. Although the crew was saved, the vessel quickly went to pieces and was a total loss. At the time of the wreck, *Daisy Rowe* was bound out of San Francisco for Coos Bay, Oregon.

Pathfinder
January 15, 1914

Since gold rush days, mariners have relied on the graceful and sturdy pilot vessel to guide their ships to a safe anchorage in San Francisco Bay. The pilots respond in all but the very worst of weather conditions, and it is a testament to their remarkable skill that more have not been lost to the hazards of navigating the Golden Gate. The pilot schooner *Pathfinder* is one of a handful of instances where a San Francisco pilot vessel was lost at sea. Built in 1900 by Matthew Turner at Benicia, California, *Pathfinder*'s schooner rig was augmented by a gasoline auxiliary engine that served well as it stayed on station on the bar, providing pilots to guide ships to the Golden Gate and into harbor.

While inbound to San Francisco in a particularly dense fog, *Pathfinder* wandered off course and ran straight into the rocks of Point Diablo, at the mid-point of the southern Marin Headlands, on the evening of January 15, 1914. In the dead of night the little vessel lay in great danger, hard against the sheer cliffs. With no chance to get ashore, the crew of five launched two small rowboats and fought their way seaward through heavy surf that threatened to pound *Pathfinder* to pieces.

By a remarkable coincidence, the crew of the nearby Point Bonita Life-Saving Station were returning in a power lifeboat from rendering assistance to a vessel in distress near Angel Island. Seeing suspicious lights near shore, they came about to investigate and ran smack into the boats from *Pathfinder*. After taking its crew on board, the life-savers came across the revenue cutter *Golden Gate*, which was searching for the overdue pilot schooner. Returning later to the scene of the wreck, the men of the Revenue Service and the Life-Saving Service, joined by the Fort Point Life-Saving Station crew, witnessed the hapless *Pathfinder* on its side, wedged onto the rocks, and full of water. Life-Saving crews and the revenue cutter *Unalaga* tried to refloat the pilot schooner the following day, but after parting a number of hawsers, *Pathfinder* was given up as a lost cause. The stranded pilot schooner quickly broke up.

Eureka
January 8, 1915

The steam schooner *Eureka* was built in 1900 at Wilmington, California for Charles P. Doe of San Francisco. Doe owned *Eureka* for twelve years, then sold it to the North Pacific Steamship Company. On January 8, 1915, the steam schooner left San Francisco, bound south for Ventura. Struck by an unusually heavy sea while in the north channel, the ship became water-logged and unmanageable. The crew abandoned ship in two small boats and were picked up by life-saving crews from the Fort Point and Point Bonita stations. Going aground within sight of the lighthouse, *Eureka* was spotted by the lighthouse keepers. Alexander Martin of the U.S. Lighthouse Service risked his life by clambering down a rope made fast to the top of the 125-foot cliff in a heroic but vain attempt to rescue survivors. Second Mate Bolger had stayed on board the crippled vessel, but his devotion cost his life, for *Eureka* drifted onto the rocks at Point Bonita and dashed to pieces.

Three Sisters
April 15, 1929

The twenty-eight-ton trawler *Three Sisters* was built in 1917 at Oakland, California, and carried a 135-horsepower diesel engine. Owned by A. Paladini of San Francisco, the vessel was a member of San Francisco's Fisherman's Wharf fishing fleet. *Three Sisters* wrecked on the rocks south of Tennessee Cove on April 15, 1929 when it ran aground at the base of Tennessee Point in a thick fog. Two of the three-man crew were killed in the surf as they struggled to reach the shore. The third man was found by the Coast Guard "on a wave beaten shelf" three hours later. He died later that evening at the hospital.

Kona
January 1, 1980

Built in 1969 at Portland, Oregon, the welded steel ocean-going barge *Kona* was valued at $2.5 million. *Kona* hauled great deckloads of general cargo between San Francisco and Hawaii. Just before midnight on December 31, 1979, *Kona* and the 400-foot-long barge *Agattu* left Oakland in tow of the 136-foot Crowley tug *Sentinal*. Their destination was Honolulu. *Kona* carried lumber, plastic pipe, and paper products. *Agattu*'s general cargo included beer, nineteen tons of nitro carbonitrate (a potentially explosive chemical used to manufacture fertilizer), and thirty-five cylinders of deadly chlorine gas.

The New Year came in with stormy weather that year. Meteorologists had predicted southwest winds to twenty knots and fifteen-foot swells. As *Sentinal* left the bay, crossed the bar, and entered the rough waters of Four Fathom Shoal, skipper John Maddux recalled that "the waves were between 35 and 40 feet high and towered over the wheelhouse of his tug." At 4 o'clock that morning the wire towline to *Kona* parted. The barge drifted out of control until it smashed on the rocky shore north of Point Bonita, between the point and Bird Rock. The surf smashed

The barge Kona, *ashore near Rodeo Lagoon on New Year's Day, 1980.*

the barge to a bent metal wreck, and scattered the cargo far and wide. All along the coast between Point Reyes and Alcatraz, flotsam from the wreck littered the shore.

Within forty minutes of *Kona's* wreck, *Agattu's* towline snagged in *Sentinel's* propeller and was cut. This even bigger barge went ashore at the south end of Cronkhite Beach, hogged, and impaled on an offshore rock. Now the threat of a widespread disaster became very real. Troops of the nearby Army posts at Fort Cronkhite and Fort Barry stayed on five-minute alert throughout that day and the next, because of the threat of exploding chlorine gas cylinders. Helicopters braved thick fog to fly over rough water and remove the dangerous cargo — without a single mishap. Salvors took the rest of *Agattu's* cargo as the water calmed and another barge came alongside. Finally *Agattu* was pulled free from the rocks. For weeks afterward, detritus from the wrecked barges littered Bay Area beaches, and scavengers collected plywood, plastic pipe, and cans of beer that had drifted far and wide in the wake of the disaster.

Chapter 5
Wrecks At Duxbury Reef And Bolinas Point

Thirteen vessels were total losses off the tiny harbor at Bolinas. The majority were lost on the rocks of Duxbury Reef, which parallels the rugged West Marin coastline for nearly a mile before jutting one thousand feet out into the Pacific at Bolinas. The reef takes its name from a near-wreck. In 1849 the ship *Duxbury*, six months out of Boston and laden with argonauts bound for the gold fields, went aground on the reef. The ship held together, and at the next high tide was pulled off by passengers and crew in the ship's boats. *Duxbury* safely made the Golden Gate and anchored off San Francisco on August 23, leaving only its name on the reef.

The editors of the San Francisco *Daily Alta California* on July 11, 1878 remarked on the danger of Duxbury Reef and the reasons for shipwrecks on it. That day they commented on the wreck of *Western Shore*, the second vessel to be lost to the reef's jagged fangs. Two steamers had been damaged, including *Prince Alfred* that sank off Tennessee Cove in June 1874 after a futile run for San Francisco.

Several sailing vessels have struck at various times. It is a very dangerous point for mariners, as there is a strong current running all the year round, which takes a vessel right on it. It is especially dreaded during the period of fogs and calms, when it has been found impossible to keep vessels out of the set, except by anchoring. Within the past month, a large English ship barely escaped loss on the reef by a lucky breeze, her stern being in but five fathoms of water when she commenced to gather way, after being anchored in the most dangerous position just clear of it for over eight hours.

Samuel S. Lewis
April 9, 1853

The screw steamer *Samuel S. Lewis* was built at Kensington (now part of Philadelphia), Pennsylvania by Theodore Birely and Son in 1851. Designed by Capt. Richard F. Loper, *Lewis* was the result of Loper's experiments with screw propulsion and marine steam engines. A practical engineer, Loper's vessels were "remarkably successful." Loper designed the steamer's engines and propeller, and supervised the hull design to "ensure that it was structurally and hydrodynamically suitable for the mode of propulsion." He personally took part in making the machinery and the hull's construction. Loper and two associates, E. Lincoln and Samuel Reynolds, intended *Lewis* to operate in the California trade, carrying immigrants and high-valued freight in the lucrative boom of steam transportation to the Pacific Coast following the discovery of California gold. But before the steamer was launched, the Harnden Express Company of Boston purchased *Lewis* to operate on the Atlantic Ocean between Boston and Liverpool.

Launched on June 12, 1851, the steamer underwent trials at Philadelphia on September 4, 1851, and sailed for Boston on September 13. Three days later *Lewis* participated in a grand jubilee on Boston harbor to celebrate the completion of the first Boston-to-Canada railroad link. At Boston, *Samuel S. Lewis* took President Millard Fillmore and other dignitaries, including Daniel Webster, on a harbor tour. *Lewis* steamed from Boston on October 4, 1851, for Liverpool, under the command of Capt. George A. Cole, recently returned from California where he had commanded the steamer *Tennessee*. *Samuel S. Lewis* was the subject of much attention and high hopes. It was not to be. At sea, *Lewis* lost the propeller in a gale and was forced to sail to Liverpool, where a new propeller was fitted. The steamer set out for Boston, only to run out of coal. Finally arriving back in the United States on January 3, 1852, *Lewis'* trans-Atlantic career ended, the owner's business having failed.

Sold in February 1852 to George A. Osgood of New York, an agent of Commodore Cornelius

Vanderbilt, *Samuel S. Lewis* was readied for a new career. Vanderbilt had established the "Independent Line" to carry gold-seekers to California by way of Nicaragua. *Lewis* was to work the Pacific side of the route with the steamer *Independence*. Steaming from New York on March 5, 1852, *Lewis* sailed into the Pacific, touching at Rio de Janeiro before navigating the Straits of Magellan. After stopping at Valparaiso and Panama, *Lewis* arrived at San Juan del Sur, the Pacific terminus of the Nicaragua route, where several hundred passangers had waited three weeks for the ship's arrival. From San Juan del Sur, *Lewis* steamed to Acapulco, Mexico, arriving at San Francisco on July 7, 1852, 112 days from New York, with 653 passengers.

The San Francisco *Daily Alta California* greeted the new steamer lukewarmly: "She is a large fine looking vessel, possessing apparently all the requisites for a good safe sea-going steamer." Vanderbilt's steamers were not noted for good service, and the death by disease of nineteen passengers enroute to San Francisco was not the best introduction for *Samuel S. Lewis*. The steamer operated between San Juan del Sur and San Francisco for more than a year, but its Pacific career was troubled, as *Lewis* ultimately contributed to the bad reputation of the Vanderbilt Line. Fined in the fall of 1852 for overloading, in January 1853 *Lewis* was described by "the most reliable authority to have arrived here in the most filthy condition; so much indeed as to create nausea to those who visited her. She is in a very leaky condition, and has several feet of water." The San Francisco *Daily Alta California*'s editors condemned the ship, stating "the lives and property of the public should not be trifled with . . . the present condition of the ship . . . is calculated to induce sickness and death, especially where human beings are packed together in dense masses. . . ."

On January 4, 1853, *Lewis* broke down off San Francisco and was towed into port by the steamer *Goliah*. A week later, the San Francisco *Daily Alta California* reported that the ship was to be "thoroughly overhauled and repaired." "New engines are going to be put in her, and new propeller paddles to replace the old ones. The copper will be stripped off, seams recaulked, new copper put on, and in time the ship made as good as new. We are really glad. . . ." The ship was repaired under contract by the Pacific Mail Steamship Company at the Benicia depot near San Francisco. The old engines were repaired, not replaced, despite the newspaper's hopes. In late March 1853 *Lewis* departed San Francisco for San Juan del Sur, only to be wrecked on the return voyage to San Francisco.

In the early morning hours of April 9, 1853, *S.S. Lewis* ran aground on Duxbury Reef, north of the point and close to Agate Beach. Thick fog obscured the land, and like the steamer *Tennessee*, lost just a month before, *Lewis* wrecked through a navigational error. William Tecumseh Sherman, (later to gain fame as a Civil War General), a passenger on board, was awakened by "a bump and sort of grating of the vessel. . . . Instantly the ship struck heavily; the engines stopped, and the running to and fro on deck showed that something was wrong." The sea was smooth and the night calm, otherwise many lives would have been lost. Nonetheless, *Lewis* rose "with the swell, and came down with a bump and quiver that was decidedly unpleasant. Soon the passengers were out of their rooms, undressed, calling for help, and praying as though the ship was going to sink immediately." The

ship did not completely sink, swinging broadside to the reef until the keel "seemed to rest on the rock and sand. At no time did the sea break over the deck—but the water below drove all the people up to the main-deck and to the promenade-deck. . . ." The officers managed to maintain order, stopping passengers who tried to lower the boats. Everyone on board waited until daybreak, when crewmembers launched a boat to find help. Gradually *Samuel S. Lewis* began to break up, "wriggling with every swell like a willow basket — the sea all around us full of the floating fragments of her sheeting, twisted and torn into a spongy condition."

The steamer's 385 passengers were safely landed on the beach along with the ship's gold shipment, mail, and some of the baggage. There bonfires were lighted to dry clothes and warm chilled passengers in the foggy morning hours. The next day the U.S. surveying steamer *Active* and the Revenue Cutter *Frolic* arrived at the scene, having first passed through a field of "drift,"

> *consisting of mattresses, benches, spars, and loose timber, which had floated down from the wreck; and what was the surprise of all on board to find that of the wreck itself, barely the hull remained! The S.S. Lewis, in one night, had completely gone to pieces! At the point on which she struck was to be seen a fragment of her hull—the lower portion—and even this remnant was being fast washed apart. Her timbers are strewn along the beach.*

All that could be saved from the ship was some passenger baggage, the gold shipment, mail, and other valuables. The steamer *Goliah* returned from the wreck site on the afternoon of April 10 with "the balance of the passengers and baggage of that vessel. Nothing now remains of the wreck together, as she has broken up, and fragments can be seen strewn all along the beach." The wreck of *S.S. Lewis* was a terrible blow to the Vanderbilt Line, costing more than $125,000 and following embarassingly close to the wreck of the Vanderbilt steamer *Independence* off Baja, California with tremendous casualties in February 1853. While the Vanderbilt Line was criticized for *Lewis'* wreck, the editors of the San Francisco *Daily Alta California* could ascertain "no charge of negligence or incapacity" toward the captain, who had been caught in unavoidable circumstances and acted responsibly in assuring the safety of his passengers after the wreck. "As there were no lives lost and no distress occasioned by this disaster, other than the temporary inconvenience to the passengers and the anxiety of their friends, this loss may be considered as rather beneficial to the traveling public than otherwise, as the *S.S. Lewis* could not be considered wholly seaworthy."

Western Shore
July 2, 1878

The 1,117-ton ship *Western Shore*, built in 1874, was the largest full-rigged vessel constructed on the Pacific Coast. The ship was 183.5 feet long with a 42-foot beam, and a 22.6-foot depth of hold, and was built of Douglas fir and Port Orford cedar. The vessel's timbers were massive with 16-by-24-inch frames. Constructed by John Kruse at Asa Meade Simpson's North Bend Shipyard at North Bend, Oregon, *Western Shore* slid off the ways on October 10, 1874.

On the maiden voyage, *Western Shore* sailed from Coos Bay to San Francisco with 225,000 board feet of lumber. At San Francisco, the vessel entered early the burgeoning California grain trade, loading wheat for Liverpool, England. Returning to San Francisco with a general cargo, it cleared for Portland, Oregon, again loading wheat for Liverpool and making a record passage of 101 days. Returning from Great Britain, *Western Shore* entered the coastal coal trade between Seattle and San Francisco. The first voyage from Seattle passed without incident, but trouble struck when the vessel sailed from San Francisco in January 1878, as the ship narrowly avoided wrecking while leaving the Golden Gate.

On January 22, *Western Shore* departed San Francisco under tow. In ballast, the lightly laden vessel proved too much for the tug *Richard Holyoke* and struggled on the line in a strong southeast gale at the Golden Gate. *Western Shore* broke free of the tug and drifted toward Alcatraz Island. "Both anchors were let go and the ship brought up, just clear of the island. Had the wind continued blowing . . . the ship must have gone ashore, but as if by a miracle it suddenly shifted . . . and the vessel was saved."

Two days later the collier again departed San Francisco under tow from the tug *Richard Holyoke*. In company of the barks *King Philip* and *Don Nicolas*, *Western Shore* was off the San Francisco Bar when the wind died. As the three vessels began to drift in heavy seas, *King Philip*'s tug cast off to aid *Western Shore* and *Don Nicolas*, both in danger of going ashore near the

The screw steamer Samuel S. Lewis, *first shipwreck on Duxbury Reef.*

The lumber schooner William F. Witzemann *on the North coast. The four-master was wrecked north of Bolinas on February 6, 1907.*

gate at Point Lobos. Capt. Blinn of *Western Shore* was casting off the tug's hawser when the wind died. He He and the mate attempted to put a few turns of the hawser around the bitts when the line surged, breaking off the bitts and striking the captain, "breaking his leg in two places, and knocking him off the forecastle to the main deck, a distance of 12 feet. . . . He lived about four hours afterwards." *Western Shore* was able to anchor and hang on until the next day, when *Richard Holyoke* hooked a line and towed the ship into San Francisco Bay. *Don Nicolas* was also towed in, but *King Philip* proved a total loss, going ashore.

Western Shore's third attempt to clear San Franciso was uneventful. However, the next voyage from Seattle to San Francisco was the last. Sailing from Seattle on July 2, 1878, the ship, laden with 2.040 tons of coal, made a fast passage toward San Francisco. On the evening of July 9, under full sail and traveling at ten knots, the ship struck *Duxbury Reef*. The lookout reported that the impact split the forefoot, throwing a large piece of it forty feet in the air. Within three hours *Western Shore* sank, lying head on, listing to port, with only the masts (all sails still set) protruding from the water. The circumstances were never fully explained.

> *There are several theories. . . . One is that there being a very strong current to the northward, the ship was considerably out of her course. Another is that the Captain, owing to a long experience, got careless. . . . Others cannot comprehend how anyone able to see either Point Reyes or Farallone light could loose a vessel on a reef so well known and dangerous as Duxbury Reef, in a fine commanding breeze. There is certainly something remarkable about the affair that needs investigation.*

The vessel, valued at $72,000, was deemed a complete loss, along with the cargo, valued at $9,180. On July 11 the "Wreck of the Ship *Western Shore*, as she now lies on Duxbury Reef," sold at auction. San Francisco grocer G. Molloy, who had earlier bought and salvaged the wrecked bark *King Philip*, now purchased the ship that had eluded disaster when *King Philip* was lost. Molloy paid $1,225 for *Western Shore;* C. Wilson separately bought the coal cargo for $70. Neither man profited, because heavy seas soon broke up the wreck. The only items salvaged were sails pulled from the yards by fishermen. Coal from the wrecked four-master washed ashore on Bolinas Beach. The late Marin County historian Jack Mason noted that as late as 1905 three hundred pound lumps of *Western Shore*'s cargo still appeared on the beach, inspiring Bolinas poet Harrison Dibblee to write, "They worked all winter till their hands were sore/Picking up coal from the *Western Shore*."

H.C. Almy
March 30, 1879

The small 12.71-ton schooner *H.C. Almy* was built by Joseph Almy at Bolinas and launched in the autumn of 1855. Almy, a sailor who had emigrated to California during the gold rush, settled in Bolinas in 1852. As master of the small schooner *Julia*, Almy carried cargoes of lumber milled at Bolinas to San

Francisco. In 1855 he decided to build his own vessel, and established a small yard on the sand spit of Stinson Beach, near the entrance to Bolinas lagoon. Almy sailed *H.C. Almy* between Bolinas and San Francisco for twelve years, carrying lumber and dairy products to market. Unfortunately, "by a series of strange mishaps, she used to get ashore nearly every trip," grounding on the sand at the entrance to the lagoon. In 1864 Almy sold her, supposedly "disgusted at the monotony of getting her away from home under such circumstances."

After 1864 *H.C. Almy* passed through a series of owners, serving at one time as a pilot schooner on the San Francisco Bar. In 1877 Capt. Mullett bought the schooner to use "in his business of catching live sea-lions." With Mullett at the helm, *H.C. Almy* sailed from San Francisco on Sunday, March 30, 1879, with a party of "twelve gentlemen, bound to the Farallones on a pleasure trip." The sea being too rough off the Farallones, Capt. Mullett ran in toward Bolinas for shelter. Arriving late in the evening, Mullett decided not to enter the narrow channel to Bolinas lagoon and anchored outside instead. The heavy surf dragged *H.C. Almy* ashore and wrecked it, "the party having a narrow escape with their lives." Mullett had not renewed the insurance policy. The sea destroyed *H.C. Almy* "only a few yards from where she was built."

Claus Spreckels

January 22, 1888

The 246-ton brigantine (later a brig) *Claus Spreckels* was built by Matthew Turner at San Francisco in 1879.

Claus Spreckels was the thirty-sixth vessel built by Turner, who constructed 228 vessels in his prodigious Pacific Coast shipbuilding career, more than any other individual nineteenth century shipbuilder in North America. *Claus Spreckels*, one of the largest two-masted vessels built on the Pacific Coast, was 122.5 feet long. Built for John D. Spreckels and Brothers, the brigantine was named for Spreckels family patriarch Claus Spreckels (1828-1908), a shrewd German immigrant who turned from the grocery business to sugar refining, gradually controlling San Francisco's sugar refineries and establishing California's sugar-beet industry. Spreckels expanded his interests to Hawaii, where he reportedly "financed the Hawaiian Kingdom and controlled much of its cane production and shipping."

Turner constructed the vessel quickly, and launched it only seventy days after the keel was laid. The San Francisco *Daily Alta California* called the ship "well built and good-looking." On its trial trip, *Spreckels* handled quite well, with builder Matthew Turner at the helm. Returning to the dock, the brigantine passed among the yachts in Raccoon Straits, and the yacht *Fleur de Lis*, racing with *Claus Spreckels*, crossed *Spreckels'* bow. Turner managed to avoid a collision, but *Claus Spreckels'* jibboom swung out and carried away *Fleur de Lis'* mainsail. The angry yachtsmen wrote a letter to the editors of the *Alta California:* "If Captain Turner possesses the preemption right to the waters of San Francisco Bay, and therewith the right to run over people, with impunity, we desire to know it, that we may govern ourselves accordingly. . . ."

After the mishap on its maiden voyage, *Claus Spreckels* cleared San Francisco for Honolulu,

The broken bow of the steam schooner R.D. Inman *frames the wreck of the four-masted schooner* Polaris *on Duxbury Reef.*

beginning a career of transporting general cargo, usually lumber, to Hawaii and bringing back sugar to San Francisco. The *Weekly Humboldt Times* of July 22, 1882, noted that *Claus Spreckels* was then "lying at Vance's wharf loading lumber for San Francisco. She will return from that city here and take a cargo of lumber to Kahalui. Captain Cousins is very proud of his vessel and counts her as one of the best sailers on the coast. She has logged 13 knots on many trips, and one trip ran the score up to 14."

Claus Spreckels wrecked on Duxbury Reef on January 22, 1888, when bound for San Francisco with $40,000 worth of sugar. As the ship approached the coast it encountered thick fog, a light east wind, and a heavy swell from the south. Running with the breeze, *Claus Spreckels* struck the reef at 4 o'clock in the morning as the watch was changing. One of the crew later stated that:

> The Captain immediately ordered out the boats and ran out the kedge with the intention of pulling her off, but the sea was too heavy and the anchor would not hold and finally between 6 and 8 o'clock we left the vessel, it being impossible to do anything with her. At the time we left her she was keeled over about 15 degrees and was full of water. . . . none of us saved anything except the clothes we had on and some few valuables we placed in our pockets.

The steamer *Emily*, bound from Ft. Bragg, rescued the ten-man crew. The tug *Relief*, dispatched to *Spreckels*, found the wreck lying on its beam ends, half full of water. *Spreckels* and the cargo were a total loss.

Esperanza
September 26, 1892

The tiny fifteen-ton, two-masted schooner *Esperanza* was built in 1877 at Capers Island, South Carolina. By 1890 *Esperanza* shifted to the Pacific Coast from its former home port of Charleston, and was running between Bolinas and San Francisco. *Esperanza* carried butter and other dairy goods from Olema Valley and Bolinas ranches to city markets, and occasionally took passengers. On September 26, 1892 *Esperanza* sailed from Bolinas with five passengers and "freight," presumably butter. Sailing from Bolinas lagoon, the schooner passed the end of Duxbury Reef, where the incoming tide caught the tiny vessel and carried it against the reef. The passengers landed safely, but "the breakers are now beating the vessel against the reef and it is expected that she will prove a total loss." *Esperanza* disintegrated in the rocks of Duxbury Reef's southernmost tip.

Nettie Low
February 7, 1900

The gold rush and the influx of a large population, the lack of local farms, factories, and ranches, and the isolation of the Pacific Coast from the rest of the

United States rendered San Francisco entirely dependent on ships for its food, particularly staples like butter, flour, vegetables, fruit, and preserves. Most of the food came from the East Coast, Hawaii, Oregon, and South America, but by 1855 the rise of farms and ranches on the Pacific Coast increased coastal trade, and by 1859 the majority of ships sailing through the Golden Gate were coasters. By the late 1850s and early 1860s, ranches and farms from the region near San Francisco supplied most of the city's dairy products and meat, particularly the Point Reyes peninsula, whose dairy farms shipped large amounts of butter, milk, cheese, and produce to market in the city.

The key to trade was the sea. Muddy, long roads from the coast stretched through hills and thick redwood forests and across streams and rivers. Rather than build better wagon roads and railroads, Point Reyes ranchers constructed small schooners that sailed from Drakes Estero forty miles down the coast, making it to the Golden Gate in a few hours. The Point Reyes schooners not only shipped ranch products to market, they also brought the feed, grain, and finery from the city. The schooners sailed every Wednesday, tide willing, and came back on Saturday.

The first schooners were small two-masted vessels less than sixty feet long. Fierce winds and the dangers of crossing the shallow, treacherous bar of the estero influenced the sailors to turn to gasoline-powered schooners that used sails when advantageous and ran their small Corliss engines to navigate the estero. The first gas-powered Point Reyes schooner was *Nettie Low*, built in 1891 and operated from San Francisco by Tom and John Low. The schooner however was substantially owned by Point Reyes

ranchers who held shares in the tiny twenty-six-ton craft.

Nettie Low made its first voyage in 1892 and was soon a regular visitor to San Francisco. In 1900, however, the vessel sailed for the last time. Departing Drakes Bay under the command of Tom Low, with engineer John Low, a seaman, and two passengers on the morning of February 7, *Nettie Low* was three miles south of Double Point just after noon when, according to Capt. Low's account in the San Francisco *Call*, "a sudden puff of wind with a twist to it like a cyclone struck the boat and careened her. She was soon on her beam ends. All of us were on deck except . . . [a passenger] . . . So slowly did the boat go over he had time to climb out and we all five scrambled on the rail. Then the lifeboat floated and we all got in and rowed ashore." The capzided schooner drifted ashore and was pounded to pieces in the rocks off Duxbury Point.

William F. Witzemann
February 6, 1907

The 473-ton four-masted schooner *William F. Witzemann* was built by Hans D. Bendixsen at Fairhaven, California and launched on March 2, 1887. Said to be the largest vessel then built on the shores of Humboldt Bay, *Witzemann* was registered at 160 feet long, with a thirty-five-foot beam. Constructed for San Francisco lumber interests, the schooner joined the Puget Sound lumber trade, ferrying lumber from Puget Sound sawmills to San Francisco markets. The cargo capacity was five hundred thousand board feet. The

Wrecks of Polaris *and* R.D. Inman *at Agate Beach.*

new schooner attracted favorable attention at the launch. "The *W.F. Witzemann* is a fine able vessel, and as she rested on the water, attracted universal attention and admiration. . . .Mr. Bendixsen is an expert shipbuilder, and the vessels constructed at his yard are considered among the best in the coasting fleet."

After a long career in the Pacific Coast lumber trade, *William F. Witzemann* wrecked three miles north of Duxbury Point on February 6, 1907. Departing San Francisco for Gray's Harbor, *William F. Witzemann*, in ballast, crashed into the rocks of Duxbury Reef in a thick fog. The five-man crew was rescued by crews from the United States Life-Saving Service's Point Bonita and Fort Point stations. The captain and two officers remained with the vessel for the next few days, superintending all possible salvage from the vessel, then abandoning the ship.

R.D. Inman
March 20, 1909

The steam schooner *R.D. Inman* was built at Marshfield, Oregon by Kruse & Banks in 1907. *R.D. Inman* was a wooden-hulled vessel registered at 768 gross tons. *R.D. Inman's* career in the Pacific Coast lumber trade was short-lived — the steam schooner was lost only two years after her launch. The ship went ashore at "Point Bolinas" on March 20, 1909, when Capt. A.J. Lancaster mistook a bonfire on the beach for the signal of a distressed ship, or a vessel adrift and on fire.

R.D. Inman had sailed in ballast from San Francisco on the evening of March 20, bound for Portland, Oregon. Darkness set in, "the sky was overcast, and there was a heavy swell from the westward." According to Capt. Lancaster,

> *When off Duxbury I saw a light inshore that looked to be from a vessel in distress, and I stood for it. The closer I got the more certain I was that it was a distressed vessel. Then it suddenly appeared that the supposed distressed vessel was on the beach, that it was a big bonfire, in fact, and before we could get out of that spot the* Inman *struck aft and stopped, and then swung inshore. The engines were reversed, but by this time the rudder-post and steering-gear broke, and the steamer began to fill.*

The engine room did not flood, and pumps kept the water level down for about an hour, until the working of the stranded steamer on the reef began to open the hull. Water overtook the pumps, drowning the fires in the boilers. *R.D. Inman* settled and washed over the reef, resting parallel to the shore five hundred feet from the beach in a shallow basin and listing heavily to starboard. The crew from the life-saving station at Point Bonita responded to the wreck but could do nothing except land the insurance company's underwriter on the beached hulk, doing their "utmost to approach the wreck" with "great skill and judgement in handling the boat in the breakers."

The vessel was wedged so tightly in the rocks that no attempt was made to free it. Owner F.S. Loop

Salvors work to remove the donkey boiler from Polaris.

of the Loop Steamship Company collected his $100,000 insurance policy. Abandoned as a total loss, *R.D. Inman* was partially salvaged by the underwriters and left to the sea. "The steamer will be stripped of machinery and deck fittings and everything of value that can be secured. It is believing that all this, however, will be worth not more than $10,000. There is no chance to save the hull." Portions of the vessel, including the bow, were still visible on the reef when the schooner *Polaris* crashed ashore near the same spot in 1914.

Polaris
January 16, 1914

The 790-ton, four-masted schooner *Polaris* was built at Marshfield, Oregon in 1902. One of a handful of Pacific Coast four-masted schooners, *Polaris* worked in the Pacific Coast lumber trade. Departing San Francisco in ballast for the northern California port of Eureka on Friday, January 16, 1914, *Polaris* crashed on rocks as a ninety-mile-an-hour gale whipped along the central coast, trapping the lighthouse keeper in his dwelling and nearly blowing the ferryboat *Thoroughfare* ashore on Yerba Buena Island. Towed out beyond the Golden Gate by the steam tug *Wilmington*, *Polaris* had been set adrift in the storm, when the towline snapped off the bar, sending both vessels adrift. *Wilmington* nearly went aground on Potato Patch Shoal before making it back into the bay. *Polaris*, the sixteen-man crew helpless, drifted north with the storm before crashing onto the rocks of Duxbury Reef at Bolinas Point. The four-master heeled to port and broke up within sight

of the remains of the steam schooner *R.D. Inman*. The vessel was partially stripped by salvors:

> *Left high and dry on the beach by the receding tide, the wrecked schooner "Polaris," which was driven ashore near Point Bolinas, has been stripped of her salvage by Captain A.S. Hansen and his crew. The schooner itself is said to be a total wreck and no effort will be made by her owners to save any of her timbers. Despite a broken back and the fact that the portions of her hull and decks were carried away in the storm, the "Polaris'" rigging was found to be practically intact.*

Before the vessel broke up, salvors took the donkey engine from *Polaris* along with the schooner's rigging.

Hanalei
November 23, 1914

The single-ended, 666-ton, wooden-hulled steam schooner *Hanalei* was built at Alameda, California, by Hay and Wright in 1901. Built for the Inter-Island Steam Navigation Co., Ltd., one of Hawaii's oldest and largest inter-island passenger and freight firms, *Hanalei* was built for trade with the island of Kauai, specifically to handle an anticipated increase in the sugar trade. *Hanalei*'s design proved unsuitable for loading sugar at Kauai and the steam schooner was not successful in the Hawaiian inter-island sugar trade. After being laid up, chartered, offered for sale, and used for emergencies, *Hanalei* was sold by Inter-Island in September 1906 for $60,000 and sent to California. The vessel ran between San Francisco and Los Angeles for two years; in 1908 the steam schooner entered the Pacific Coast lumber trade, carrying lumber and passengers between San Francisco and various north coast ports.

Sailing from Eureka, California with sixty-two persons on board and a cargo of lumber, live cattle, sheep, and hogs, *Hanalei* was lost on November 23, 1914 when nearing the Golden Gate. The steam schooner ran aground on Duxbury Reef opposite the Marconi Wireless Station in Bolinas around noon on Monday, November 23. Thick fog obscured the water. The steamer struck the rocks without warning, tearing off the rudder. Stuck on the rocks, *Hanalei* remained in the surf for eighteen hours as rescuers, alerted by the ship's wireless SOS, gathered on shore. Efforts to rig a breeches buoy failed, and two crewmembers who tried to swim a line ashore drowned in the surf. As night fell, would-be rescuers lit bonfires on the beach to wait for morning. When *Hanalei* disintegrated, passengers and crew were thrown into the surf. The wreckage and the loose lumber cargo, as well as the choking effect of the ship's leaking diesel fuel took a deadly toll: twenty-three persons, including eighteen passengers, died as they struggled to reach the shore. The life-saving steamer *McCulloch*'s crew plucked a few survivors from the water; others, including a small boy, washed alive to the beach after several hours in the water, buoyed by floating wreckage.

Hanalei was the worst shipwreck disaster on Duxbury Reef. Efforts to save the shipwreck victims had been considerable. "Ineffectual attempts were repeatedly made by the life-savers on shore to shoot a line across to the doomed vessel while yet she held together. Several tugs and government vessels likeways essayed long in vain to get near enough to rescue the people on board, the seas breaking over the reef with fearful force." *Hanalei* was destroyed by the surf, breaking into splinters. A large fragment of the hull washed in close to shore with some survivors clinging to it; that section was the only part of *Hanalei* visible when the surf subsided.

Criticism of Capt. J.J. Carey was immediate. One newspaper openly stated, "The wrecking of the *Hanalei* seems to have been due to the negligence of her officers. . . ." Capt. Carey, who had been below when the ship crashed, blamed the disaster on first mate W.C. Reese, who had perished in the wreck. A Board of Inquiry found Capt. Carey guilty of negligence, and suspended his master's license.

Acalin
August 30, 1934

The eighty-seven-ton, diesel-powered *Acalin* was built at Los Angeles in 1928. The purse-seiner's wooden hull was seventy-three feet long. Home-ported in San Pedro, *Acalin* ranged up and down the coast from Baja California to Point Reyes. *Acalin*'s fishing career was uneventful until 1933, when Capt. Jerry Acalin, brother of the vessel's owner, and two members of the crew were accused of killing Mexican customs guard Pedro Gonzales Pineda off Ensenada, Mexico. The incident sparked an international controversy between the United States and Mexico, and Acalin and his two

Polaris.

accomplices were convicted of manslaughter and sentenced to eighteen months at the United States Penitentiary on McNeil Island, Washington.

The next major event in *Acalin's* career occurred the following year on Duxbury Reef. On August 30, 1934, the seiner, with owner Frank Acalin in command, was returning to San Francisco after delivering supplies to the steamer *Lansing*, which lay at anchor between Bolinas and Point Reyes. In the darkness of the early morning, Capt. Acalin ran the vessel close in to the shore through thick fog. Just off Duxbury Reef, *Acalin* struck the reef's edge, the rocks tearing holes in the bow and side. As water poured in, Capt. Acalin pulled the vessel off the rocks and began to run for shore. The crew fired a gun, set off flares, and ignited pitch and fuel oil on deck to signal for help. As *Acalin* rounded the reef, whistle blowing and engine room quickly flooding, the hapless purse-seiner sank. *Acalin* beached it "on the sandy shore at the south end of the reef" and the ten-man crew took to the boats. As they reached shore they met the crew from the United States Coast Guard Station at Bolinas, who had been alerted by the sinking vessel's signals.

The Red Stack tug *Sea King* raced to salvage *Acalin* but gave it up. "The only visible vestige of the vessel was a stubby mast sticking out of the water." *Acalin* could not be pulled free, despite several attempts. The hulk, imbedded in the south end of the reef, was deemed a hazard to small craft traffic, and on January 1, 1935 the Coast Guard crew from the Bolinas Station "placed a charge of TNT in the hulk and blew the vessel to bits."

San Domenico
December 27, 1935

The eighty-six-foot-long purse-seiner *San Domenico* was built at San Francisco by Andersen & Cristofani and was launched in September 1935. *San Domenico* was built for and owned by the vessel's crew. The purse-seiner's career was brief. Just three months after its launch, *San Domenico* wrecked four miles north of Bolinas, running aground in heavy fog on December 27, 1935. The hull torn open by rocks, *San Domenico* filled with water as the eleven-man crew lowered a skiff and headed for shore through the surf. Struggling to reach the beach, a quarter-mile distant from the wreck, most of the crew made it, but one man, Salvatore Finocchiaro, was swept overboard and drowned. The wreck quickly broke up in the heavy surf. Nothing was saved, and Finocchiaro's body was never found.

YFD #20
January 20, 1943

Built in 1942 for the United States Navy, the steel-hulled Yard Floating Drydock #20 was small for a floating drydock, its 622 feet capable of lifting only sixty-five hundred tons. YFD #20 was being delivered to the Navy when the tow line parted and the drydock grounded on the rocks of Duxbury Reef on January 20, 1943. A major storm lashing the coast between January 18 and 22 was the major cause of the wreck. The Navy

The steam schooner Hanalei, *Duxbury Reef's worst maritime disaster. The November 23, 1914 wreck took 23 lives.*

The stranded hull of the purse seiner Acalin *at the mouth of Bolinas Bay. The 87-ton vessel was blown apart as a hazard to navigation.*

scrapped the stranded drydock over the next month, but because of wartime censorship no mention was made, and YFD #20 was quietly stricken from the Navy's records.

The force of the waves that tore apart the steamer Tennessee is graphically shown on this piece of iron boiler plating recovered by National Park Service archeologists in 1983.

Conclusion
Discovering The Wrecks

Deep waters, swift currents, rocky shorelines, and thick, shrouding beach sands have obscured most traces of shipwrecks in the Gulf of the Farallones. Treacherous diving conditions keep all but the most skilled divers out of the water. At slack tide when the currents slow, divers have visited the wrecks of *City of New York, Samuel S. Lewis, and Ohioan,* and have surveyed the bottom of Tennessee Cove looking for submerged wreckage from *S.S. Tennessee.* The blasted remains of *Benevolence* appear on navigational charts, and the stern of *Puerto Rican,* holding as much as 11,725 barrels of bunker fuel, was located in 1,246 feet of water off the Farallon Islands.

Most vessels have not been seen or visited since they wrecked. Given harsh conditions, their discovery depends on deliberate search rather than chance encounter. Sport divers interested in the history of the wrecks have done considerable research, but for the most part shipwreck work off the Golden Gate has been done by the National Park Service. Archaeological survey and evaluation by the National Park Service and others have found and identified shipwrecks, including *S.S. Tennessee, Neptune, King Philip, Reporter,* and *Atlantic's* remains on the beaches of San Francisco and Marin counties. Pieces of *S.S.*

Tennessee's sidelever engine and paddlewheels lie on the beach of Tennessee Cove and are occasionally exposed when winter storms strip the sand away. In 1880 historian J.P. Munro-Fraser described a paddlewheel shaft sticking out of the surf. Another piece constantly exposed is a massive cast-and-wrought-iron crosstail that lies near the cliff's edge at the southern edge of the cove. The crosstail, a connecting link in the engine between the sidelevers and the paddlewheel shafts, weighs more than a ton. It was snapped off by the force of the ocean and washed up onto the beach by heavy surf that tore *Tennessee* apart.

Archaeological excavation by the National Park Service, the Miwok Archaeological Preserve of Marin, and the *S.S. Tennessee* Archaeological Project, Inc. between 1980 and 1981 found dozens of pieces of the steamer: fastenings that held together *Tennessee's* oak timbers, cast-iron engine parts, a piece of wrought-iron boiler plating, torn pieces of copper sheathing, and sheathing nails by the hundreds scattered in pockets of rocks beneath the sand. The sheathing and nails are graphic evidence of the wreck, proving the *Alta's* March 7, 1853 claim, "her copper is much chafed and rubbed off." Some of *Tennessee's* provisions were found: a shattered piece of crockery that probably held butter, a fluted bottle fragment, and a liquor bottle base. Deep sand in the cove covers the broken bottom and large pieces of the engine; underwater excavation in the heavy surf is required before more of *Tennessee* is revealed. The crosstail is frequently exposed on the beach and can be seen through the winter, its rusting arms thrust into the pebbles and sand of the beach.

In the last weeks of 1982, gale-force winds, combined with extremely high tides, lashed the California coast, sweeping large amounts of sand to sea. On Ocean Beach in San Francisco, the beach dropped between one and one-half to nine feet and receded nearly sixty-four feet. The loss of sand stripped the beach at Fort Funston down to a rocky substrata, exposing the remains of a wooden vessel lying on the rocks and nestled against the cliffs. The seven-by-forty-eight-foot section of hull lay directly beneath the Fort Funston overlook and close to where hang gliders launch to ride the winds that sweep up the 130-foot tall cliffs.

The National Park Service and volunteers cleaned and documented the exposed hull, which proved to be nearly half of a small wooden sailing vessel of the late nineteenth century. The section included the intact side of the hull from the turn of the bilge to the level of the main deck. The knees that once supported the deck had been torn free, leaving only fragments of the "hold-beam-shelf," a long timber in the hold. No bottom timbers were found, indicating that the side had torn free. The stubs of flat, wrought-iron chainplates that once held rigging, were still attached to the hull's outer planks.

Hull measurements indicated the vessel was originally around one hundred feet in length, with a 9-foot depth of hold. Built entirely of Douglas fir, the vessel was probably constructed on the Pacific coast. Douglas fir was used exclusively for shipbuilding on the Pacific coast after 1860, replacing more expensive Eastern hardwoods. Douglas fir was particularly used to build vessels for the lumber trade because it was durable, cheap, and locally available. The style of construction and fastenings also indicated a late nineteenth century date of construction very similar to the three-masted 1895 lumber schooner *C.A. Thayer*, a National Historic Landmark vessel moored at Hyde Street Pier in San Francisco Maritime National Historical Park. Working with Naval architect and historian Ray Aker of Palo Alto and shipwreck historian Max O'Starr of Pacifica, National Park Service archaeologists identified the remains as the two-masted schooner *Neptune*, lost at the site on August 10, 1900. Photographs of *Neptune*'s wreck showed the schooner on the beach against the cliffs of Fort Funston, and newspaper accounts and the official report of the United States Life-Saving Service placed the schooner within one thousand feet of the location of the exposed wreckage.

The estimated size of the wrecked vessel closely fits *Neptune*'s rather than the only other vessel known to have been lost there, the 1863-built *William Frederick*, a much smaller ship. The similarity of construction technique between *Neptune* and *C.A. Thayer* was no coincidence. They were both built by Hans Bendixsen at Fairhaven, near Eureka, within thirteen years of each other. Bendixsen used proven models of hull design. An account of a ship launching at his yard in 1895 noted that "the model of the *C.A. Thayer* and *Maeweema* seems to be a favorite one, as Mr. Bendixsen has the keel laid at his yard for a third schooner on the same lines." Likewise, it seems, Bendixsen also employed the same successful, standard shipbuilding techniques and methods. On August 12, 1900, after the last attempt to pull the stranded *Neptune* off the beach failed, the tugs departed, "leaving the ill-fated vessel to bleach its bones on the beach," according to the *San Francisco Chronicle*. As the winter storms of 1982 proved, *Neptune* did just that. Now reburied by shifting sands, its remains have not been seen again.

The same winter storm that exposed the remains of *Neptune* also pulled enough sand off Ocean Beach at the foot of Ortega Street to reveal the timbers from another wreck's bow. Further erosion of the beach in 1983 exposed the complete outline of the bow and stern, allowing National Park Service archaeologists and volunteers to determine the length and beam of the vessel. The construction method, size, and location of the remains indicated it could only be the bark *King Philip*, lost there on January 25, 1878 after going ashore in a gale. The bow timbers included a breasthook, which is a diagonally-set timber that reinforces the bow. Carved or branded into the wood was a "W." The "W" does not match any known shipwright's mark used to label timbers, but it could conceivably come from the name of Dennett Weymouth, the Maine shipbuilder who constructed *King Philip* on the banks of the Sheepscot River in 1856.

After being reburied by beach sand in the summer of 1983, winter storms in early 1984 again exposed *King Philip*. In April and May the sand washed out from around the wreck, exposing the entire outline of the ship. The sides, broken down to a level three to five feet lower than the more heavily

The nearly intact bottom of the ship King Philip, *exposed by winter storms on Ocean Beach, 1984.*

The stern of King Philip. The ship separated at the lower or 'tween deck level where salvors blasted the ship apart in 1878.

built bow and stern, had not been seen earlier. The wreck's port side, facing offshore, could be worked only by divers. The sheathing remained attached to the hull; analysis proved it to be Muntz metal, a composite also known as Naval brass or "yellow metal" that came into common use after 1860. Two knees from the lower of *King Philip*'s two decks survived at the stern. The knees and measurements of the depth of the wreckage, which ran from the buried keel some sixteen feet to the top of the exposed stem and sternposts, indicated that nearly half of the ship's hull lay on the beach. *King Philip* lies canted to port, battered by waves on the port side. The hull is separated at the level of the 'tweendeck, a logical breaking place when the ship was blasted apart by salvor John Molloy in 1878. The interior of *King Philip*'s hull is filled with stone ballast as the ship carried no cargo at the time of the wreck, being bound north to load lumber.

When the beach dropped a few more feet, archaeologists found an iron turnbuckle, a lead pipe from a scupper or a "soil pipe" from the head, and several sections of wire rope draped around the bow. These pieces, it was felt, were deposited on the site after *King Philip*'s loss, since all of the ship's rigging had been salvaged by Molloy and these pieces were apparently deposited on the broken hulk after that effort. The exposure of large iron drifts and other ship fastenings, as well as pieces of Douglas fir inshore of the wreck and a small set of bobstays, indicated yet another ship lay at the site. Bobstays are chains and deadeyes that connect the bowsprit and the stem. Acting much like a turnbuckle, bobstays pull down, while martingale stays pull from the sides and a triatic stay pulls up. The tension of the stays holds the bowsprit rigid.

The bobstays, iron drifts (*King Philip* was copper-fastened), turnbuckle, and Douglas fir timbers could come from only one wreck — the three-masted lumber schooner *Reporter*, built on the Pacific coast in 1876 and lost next to *King Philip* on March 13, 1902. A magnetometer, an instrument that measures the magnetic "signature" of buried objects, scanned the *King Philip* site and traced a large buried mass off the ship's exposed bow. This mass and the scattered wreckage on the sand represent the broken and scattered remains of *Reporter*. The wire rope had been used to rig *Reporter*; the tangled strands in *King Philip*'s bow probably are the shrouds from *Reporter*'s mizzenmast, which toppled in the surf across *Philip*'s exposed remains. When abandoned to the surf, the broken hulk of *Reporter* was described as "fast digging her own grave alongside the bones of the *King Philip*, whose ribs are still seen. . ." The two wrecks remain buried side by side. Archaeologists moved the scattered pieces of *Reporter* to the National Maritime Museum in 1984, but its buried hull lies too deep to be exposed. *King Philip* occasionally can be seen during winter storms, lying in the surf at the foot of Ortega Street.

Two archaeological surveys of Ocean Beach were done using magnetometers. The first, a cooperative venture by the National Park Service, the Nautical Heritage Museum of Dana Point, California, and the U.S. Coast Guard, focused on the waters and beach off the foot of Sloat Street. There in 1851 the U.S. Revenue Marine brig *C.W. Lawrence* was lost. On November 28, 1851, the *Alta California* reported that the pilot boat *Rialto*'s crew had seen *Lawrence* "with the crew stripping her of yards, masts, and rigging. They have a tent on shore close to the wreck, which lays about four miles southward of Point Lobos." Based on historical accounts, including *Lawrence*'s log and an 1852 Coast Survey chart that shows a wreck on the beach, a half-mile-square area was selected. The Nautical Heritage Museum helped fund the survey to locate the Revenue brig's remains, since the vessel had inspired their tallship *Californian,* now the state's sailing goodwill ambassador and youth sail-training vessel.

Using a Coast Guard vessel, Park Service archaeologists towed a magnetometer through the water to locate any wreckage that lay submerged or in the surf zone. The survey also extended onto the beach, which was carefully gridded into sections and surveyed, with the magnetometer taking a reading every six feet. Heavy fog and five-to-eight-foot swells breaking inside the survey area compounded the difficulty. The Coast Guard boat's commander, coxswain Gregory Gordon, and crewmembers Lisa McDade and Tracey Brown, literally surfed the boat in and out of the survey zone while the magnetometer operator took his readings. Despite the difficulties, the magnetometer located a buried mass in surf zone that could be wreckage from *Lawrence,* the schooner *Aimer,* or the three-masted schooner *William L. Beebe.* All three vessels had wrecked in the project area, *Aimer* in 1871 and *Beebe* in 1894. Diving the "target" was impossible because of the heavy surf. The magnetometer detected numerous targets on the beach, which could be scattered debris from the three wrecks that washed ashore. Only excavating the deep

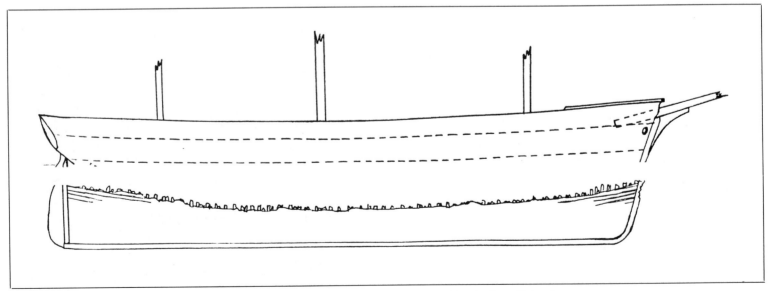

Side view sketch of King Phillip. The top of the ship wore away over time leaving what is shown at the bottom, buried on Ocean Beach near Noriega Street.

beach sands will reveal exactly what the magnetometer found.

A second beach survey with the magnetometer proved more successful. The City of San Francisco's Cleanwater Program's plans to build a reinforced concrete seawall along Ocean Beach in the vicinity of the wrecks of *King Philip* and *Reporter* led to a survey of that section of the beach. The survey was required by the National Park Service because the construction of the seawall would disturb areas on the beach within the boundaries of the Golden Gate National Recreation Area. Since the *King Philip* and *Reporter* wrecks are listed in the National Register of Historic Places, the survey was required to see if areas of the two wrecks, or any others, would be disturbed by the seawall construction. If that was found to be the case, then plans to protect the wrecks or limit the disturbance to a minimum could be prepared.

The survey was done under contract to the city by Espey, Huston and Associates of Austin, Texas. Espey, Huston has done other shipwreck surveys and work throughout the United States, including an archaeological survey on the Sacramento River that discovered the remains of two gold rush shipwrecks. Under the supervision of EH&A archaeologist Robert L. Gearhart, the survey team carefully gridded the beach and surveyed an area from Noriega street to Rivera street in 1987. The magnetic contour of the wrecks of *King Philip* and *Reporter* was delineated. What may be the contours of two other wrecks was also recorded, one of which lies close to the reported location of the 1886 wreck of the whaling bark *Atlantic*, the worse maritime disaster on Ocean Beach. The

survey indicated that buried wreckage from *King Philip* and *Reporter* was not likely to lie in the area of seawall construction. Scattered wreckage from the supposed *Atlantic* site did, however, and in the summer of 1987 EH&A archaeologists excavated a magnetic reading on the beach. The excavation disclosed a buried section of the ship's keel, a massive oak timber sheathed with copper. The only copper-sheathed wreck within a mile of the area was *Atlantic*, so it seems that some of the scattered wreckage came from the ill-fated whaling bark that disintegrated in the surf and spread along the beach, killing thirty-two men.

The most recent shipwreck survey was done quietly by members of a Bay Area family. Searching in the deep waters of the channel off the Golden Gate, the family of the late Adm. William Gibson used side-scan

The crosstail from Tennessee's engine, lying on the beach at Tennessee cove, 1980.

sonar to find the sunken hulk of *City of Rio de Janeiro*, whose remains have proved elusive since the 1901 wreck of the steamer. The first attempt to locate *City of Rio de Janeiro* began immediately after the sinking. In 1901 the "Rio Wrecking Company" was formed to find and salvage the wrecked steamer. According to the company's prospectus, on March 14, 1901, less than three weeks after the disaster, "Capt. John Ross, assisted by Capt. J.J. Sullivan, in company with submarine divers Thomas Olsen and John McLaughlin, began the search in the harbor of San Francisco. . . ." Their goal was the rich cargo; $1,200,000 worth of "silk, opium, coconut oil, tin" and was further spurred by "rumors of treasure." *Rio de Janeiro* carried $20,000 for the steamer's own use. The Collector of Customs at Honolulu shipped $35,000 in gold, which was insured by Newhall & Co. of San Francisco. The rumors of treasure concerned $250,000 in gold coin shipped in the lost steamer to San Francisco banks.

The Rio Wrecking Company said, "We feel perfectly safe . . . in stating . . . that we think we have located the wreck of the steamship *Rio* in 21 to 23 fathoms of water [140 feet] where the sea is rough and choppy, the currents strong, and where diving will be difficult." The company failed to back up its claim. After 1901, numerous searches and occasional "discoveries" of the wreck were announced. In 1913 diver Herman Stelzner, "inventor of a new diving device, went down 128 feet. . . in the vicinity of Mile Rock, and saw the shadow of a hull which he believes to be the remains of the . . . *Rio de Janeiro*. . . . The *Rio*'s cargo included a large shipment of raw silk, the value of which is doubtful after 12 years submersion. There was also a shipment of tin, which might be worth recovering. . . . The only money known to be

on board is locked up in the purser's safe."

In May 1924 the Army Corps of Engineers' dredge *Culebra*, deepening the San Francisco channel five miles west of the Golden Gate, struck an obstruction thought to be *City of Rio de Janeiro*. The wreck was again "located" in 1937 by Santa Barbara diver Bill Wood, who claimed he found the steamer lying bottom up in the shallows between Mile Rock and Land's End with holes in the hull "big enough to pass a railcar through." Wood claimed to have a lifeboat plaque that read "Rio de Janeiro — Capacity 20 Persons," but said he made no attempt to salvage the wreck because "she contained nothing of value." However, newspaper reports of Wood's "discovery" noted that "there have been persistent reports over the years . . . that the vessel carried $5,000,000 in gold into the murky depths of the Golden Gate." The same year, 1937, retired United States Postal Inspector William Ives Madeira claimed to have deposited $75,000 in gold aboard the steamer while it stopped at Honolulu enroute to San Francisco. While doing so, he claimed, he saw stacks of ingots in the hold that a crewmember said was "Chinese silver" worth $2,000,000. Madeira's claim spurred other efforts to locate *City of Rio de Janeiro*.

In May 1946, a highly publicized hunt for the wreck one and one-half miles southwest of Mile Rock led to the discovery of a wreck near Seal Rocks. The diving group searching for *Rio de Janeiro* dug into the sand, found a wooden-hulled wreck and abandoned their efforts. In 1955 another group claimed to have found the wreck lying in one hundred feet of water inside the bay off Angel Island. The divers reported making daily dives on the wreck, searching for a precious cargo they believed to be "at least $2,000,000 in gold bars and bullion, silver and gems." Nothing came of this quest. Also in the 1950s, Oakland diver Al Mikalow began to search for *Rio de Janeiro* off Angel Island. In May 1985 he again stated his plans to excavate the wreck, explaining "I've been chasing the *Rio* since 1950 . . . I know it's in there. It's taken this long to build the proper equipment and raise enough money . . ." Five months later, the Gibson family consortium, incorporated as "Seagamb, Inc." (for sea gamble) petitioned the California State Lands Commission for a permit to survey the wreck and salvage the silver bullion William Ives Madeira claimed he saw. Seagamb offered as evidence a side-scan sonar image that clearly shows a large steamship, substantially intact, with a profile that strikingly matches *Rio de Janeiro*, lying in the channel in three hundred feet of water. Seagamb also provided detailed historical research, and used tidal and current data as well to reconstruct the wreck event that makes a compelling case for the ship striking at Lime Point and sinking just to the north of mid-channel in the deepest waters of the Golden Gate. The evidence was sufficient to list the shipwrecked remains of *City of Rio de Janeiro* in the National Register of Historic Places in 1988. Seagamb, intensely interested in the history of the elusive steamer, is uncertain whether Madeira's treasure is aboard. In any case, their efforts resolved one of the Golden Gate's most intriguing mysteries, and marked the resting place of San Francisco's "Titanic" on the map.

The graves of many other wrecks at the Golden Gate have always been known and can be seen by the most casual observer. In addition to the occasionally exposed remains of *Tennessee* and *King Philip*, wreckage from four other vessels is usually visible year 'round. At Land's End in San Francisco, visitors hiking along the trail can see the boilers and sternpost of *Ohioan* between Point Lobos and the sea stacks to the north of the point. *Ohioan*'s remains lie in thirty-six feet of water and run in to the rocky shore, where beachcombers at low tide see torn sections of double-riveted steel plates, deck beams, frames, and at least one bitt from the freighter's forecastle deck. The ship split into three sections; the bow, now disintegrated, lies close to shore and on the beach. The midships section, including the engine room, lies in deeper water and is marked by the boilers, whose rounded tops spout like whales when the surf rolls through them. The stern lies in deeper water, and the stern post sticks up close to the rocks of Point Lobos, visible from the overlook atop the point.

Just around the bend and north of Point Lobos lie the remains of *Frank H. Buck* and *Lyman Stewart*. Buck's triple expansion steam engine sticks above the water close to a finger of rock that reaches down from the cliffs and ends yards away from the tanker's engine and the rudderpost. The hull lies torn open and runs deep into the channel, ending at the bow more than a hundred feet down. Close by, and immediately to the east, lies the exposed triple expansion engine of *Buck*'s sister ship, *Lyman Stewart*. Battered and torn apart by the surf as it lies parallel to the shore, *Stewart*'s hull is spread throughout the cove with pieces lying in the surf.

Farther east, but just west of China Beach, the scrapped and scanty steel remains of *Coos Bay* are exposed by extremely low tides on the rocks where the freighter ran aground in 1927. Rangers from the Ocean District of the Golden Gate National Recreation Area

The starboard side of the hull of the schooner Neptune *at Fort Funston, 1982.*

offer a "Landslides and Shipwrecks" walk around Land's End on most weekends. The Rangers tell the stories of the wrecks and point out the remains of *Ohioan, Buck, Stewart* and, when visible, *Coos Bay*. On the other side of the Gate, GGNRA's rangers from the Marin Headlands district offer an occasional Tennessee Valley walk that ends at the beach of the cove and, if the tide is right and the sand is washed away, pieces of *Tennessee*.

The compelling story of the wrecks at the Golden Gate unfolds in a variety of ways. New technology makes shipwrecks easier to find, as the discovery of *Titanic* and *City of Rio de Janeiro* demonstrates. Nearly all the wrecks discussed and described lie within the boundaries of either the Golden Gate National Recreation Area and the Gulf of the Farallones National Marine Sanctuary. Both the National Park Service, which hosts the federal government's only field team of underwater archaeologists (the Submerged Cultural Resource Unit) and the National Oceanic and Atmospheric Administration plan to survey shipwrecks in the future, hoping to locate, study, and present to the public unique and fascinating stories gleaned from the shattered, submerged bones of the shipwrecks of the Golden Gate.

Clipper card advertising King Philip, *circa 1860.*

Appendix 1:
Characteristics Of The Shipwrecked Vessels

NAME	BUILT	WRECKED	TYPE/RIG	MASTS	L B D	GROSS
Aberdeen	1847	1852	Ship	3	154x32.4x16.2	719
Aberdeen	1899	1916	Steam Schr	2	169.8x34.2x11.8	499
Acalin	1928	1934	Purse Seiner	-	73x18.7x8.6	87
Aimer	1870	1871	Schooner	2	86x26x5	96
American Boy	1882	1890	Schooner	2	105.6x31.5x8.5	183
Ann Parry	1825	1865	Bark	3	107x27x13.1	348
Annie Sisie	1856	1871	Ship	3	180x39.1x23	1163
Atlantic	1851	1886	Bark	3	116.9x26.3x13.1	366
Beeswing	?	1863	Schooner	2	Unknown	---
Benevolence	1944	1950	C-4 Frghtr.	2	520x71.6x24	11,141
Bessie Everding	1876	1888	Schooner	2	73.5x25.5x6.5	73
Bonita	1892	1900	Pilot Schr	2	88x23x9.8	75
Bremen	1858	1882	Ship	3	328x40.2x33.4	2687
Brignardello	1865	1868	Bark	3	Unknown	543
C.W. Lawrence	1848	1851	Brig	2	96.5x24	144
Caroline Amelia	?	1850	Bark	3	Unknown	---
Champlain	1874	1875	Ship	3	216x40x24	1473
Chateau Palmer	1855	1856	Ship	3	Unknown	800
City of Chester	1875	1888	Steamer	2	202x33.2x15.9	1106
City of New York	1875	1893	Steamer	2	339x40.2x28.9	3019
City of Rio	1878	1901	Steamer	2	345x38.6x19.9	3548
Claus Spreckels	1879	1888	Brig	2	122.5x31.8x10.5	246
Coos Bay	1909	1927	Freighter	-	386x53x29.8	5451
Daisy Rowe	1879	1900	Schooner	2	94.5x29x7.5	122
Dublin	1839	1882	Bark	3	139x30.8x22	706
Eliza	1868	1871	Sloop	1	Unknown	10.20
Elizabeth	1882	1891	Ship	3	231.5x41.8x19.8	1866
Elko	1868	1881	Scow Schr	2	96.5x32x6	147
Escambia	1879	1882	Steamer	-	291x34.7x24.5	2154

Esperanza	1877	1892	Schooner	2	46.2x15.8x3.5	15
Eureka	1868	1902	Schooner	3	134.3x33x10.5	295
Eureka	1900	1915	Steam Schr	2	142.5x26x12	484
F.W. Bailey	1854	1863	Ship	3	160x33.3x21.6	711
Franconia	1874	1881	Ship	3	207.6x40.6x23	1461
Frank Jones	1874	1877	Ship	3	203x40x24	1452
Frank H. Buck	1914	1937	Tanker	-	408.8x55.5x31.7	6076
General Cushing	1856	1858	Ship	3	150x31.5x15.8	681
George Louis	1863	1882	Schoone	2	60.7x21.3x5.6	40
Gifford	1892	1903	Bark	4	281.6x42.3x24.6	2245
Golden Fleece	1852	1854	Clipper	3	173x35x21	968
Granada	1855	1860	Steamer	-	228x31x15.6	1058
H.C. Almy	1855	1879	Schooner	2	36x13x4.4	12
H.L. Rutgers	1855	1868	Bark	3	167x36.5x22.5	405
Hanalei	1901	1914	Steam Schr	2	174.5x36x13	666
Helen W. Almy	1859	1898	Bark	3	117x29x12.9	314
Henry Bergh	1943	1944	EC-2 Frghtr.	-	441.6x57x37.4	7176
Isaac Jeanes	1854	1876	Bark	3	157x35x21	814
Jenny Ford	1854	1864	Barkentine	3	133.4x30.3x10.1	397
Josephine Wilcutt	1860	1872	Schooner	2	80x26x6.5	86
Julia Castner	1858	1859	Bark	3	142x29x13.4	509
King Philip	1856	1878	Bark	3	186.6x37.2x24	1194
Kona	1969	1980	Barge	-	336.3x98x20.2	5825
Labouchere	1858	1866	Steamer	-	190x26.1x14.9	507
Louis	1888	1907	Schooner	5	193.8x36x18	831
Lyman A. Stewart	1914	1922	Tanker	-	408.8x55.5x31.7	6076
Lucas	1828	1858	Ship	3	102x25x12	---
Mersey	1840	1850	Bark	3	Unknown	393
Morning Light	1858	1868	Schooner	2	60x20x5.8	43
Neptune	1882	1900	Schooner	2	106x29x8.5	184
Nettie Low	1891	1900	Schooner	2	55x18.5x4.6	26
Noonday	1854	1863	Clipper	3	200x38.6x23.6	1189
Ohioan	1914	1936	Freighter	-	407.7x53.7x28.1	5135
Palestine	1877	1891	Ship	3	209.4x40x23.9	1397
Parallel	1868	1887	Schooner	2	98x31x8	148
Pathfinder	1900	1914	Pilot Schr	2	81x24x9.5	86
Patrician	1859	1873	Ship	3	195x35.7x22.5	1140
Pet	1868	1888	Schooner	2	67.5x22x5.5	49

Petersburg	1837	1852	Schooner	2	81.6x25.6x10.4	183
Prince Alfred	1852	1874	Steamer	-	160.5x32.7x21.9	815
Polaris	1902	1914	Schooner	4	195.1x40x15.6	790
Puerto Rican	1971	1984	Tanker	-	632.3x90x45.8	20,295
R.D. Inman	1907	1909	Steam Schr	2	186.5x39x14	768
Reporter	1876	1902	Schooner	3	141.4x34x10.6	351
Rescue	1865	1874	Tug	-	100x25x12	139
Robert Henderson	1838	1850	Bark	3	Unknown	368
Samson	1890	1895	Schr Barge	2	109x34x8	21
Samuel S. Lewis	1851	1853	Steamer	3	216.9x32.6x16.3	1103
San Domenico	1935	1935	Purse Seiner	-	86x?x?	---
San Francisco	1853	1853	Clipper	3	198x38x22	1307
Schah Jehan	?	1867	Ship	3	Unknown	---
Tagus	?	1851	Ship	3	Unknown	---
Tennessee	1848	1853	Steamer	3	211.1x35.8x22	1275
Three Sisters	1917	1929	Trawler	-	56.3x15.6x6	28
Unnamed Scow	?	1892	Scow	-	Unknown	---
Viscata	1864	1868	Ship	3	204x32.8x21.6	1065
W.H. Gawley	1861	1880	Barkentine	3	147x31.7x17	483
Western Shore	1874	1878	Ship	3	183x42x22	1117
Wm. F. Witzemann	1887	1907	Schooner	4	160x35x12.2	473
William Frederick	1863	1887	Schooner	2	63x22x4	42
William L. Beebe	1875	1894	Schooner	3	134.7x33.3x10.7	296
William Mighel	?	1873	Schooner	2	?x?x?	25
YFD #20	1942	1943	Floating Drydock		622x124	6500
Yosemite	1906	1926	Steam Schr	2	193x40x10.6	827
Zenobia	1838	1858	Ship	3	143.9x33.1x15.5	630

NOTE: In most cases the gross tonnage has been rounded and does not reflect the lesser percentage, i.e. "40/95."

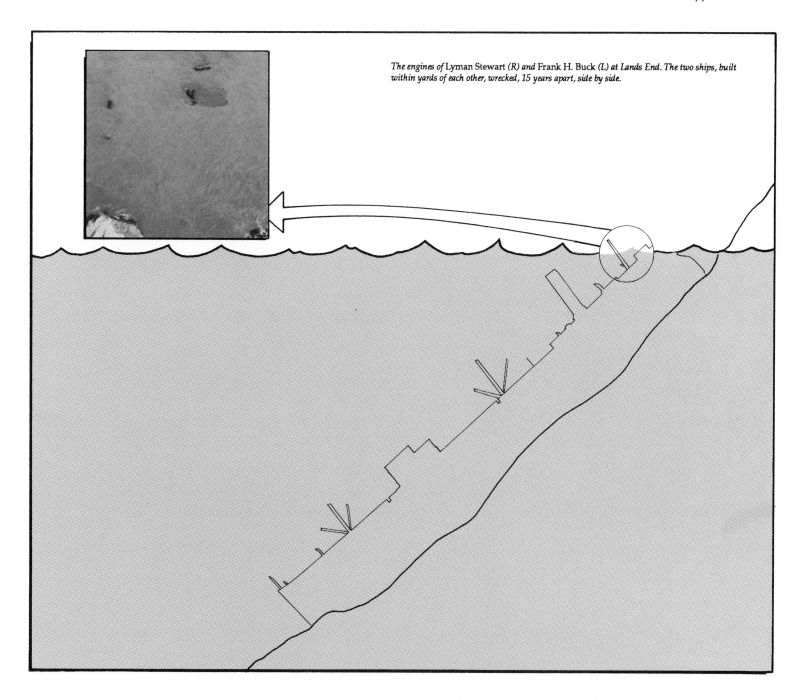

The engines of Lyman Stewart *(R) and* Frank H. Buck *(L) at Lands End. The two ships, built within yards of each other, wrecked, 15 years apart, side by side.*

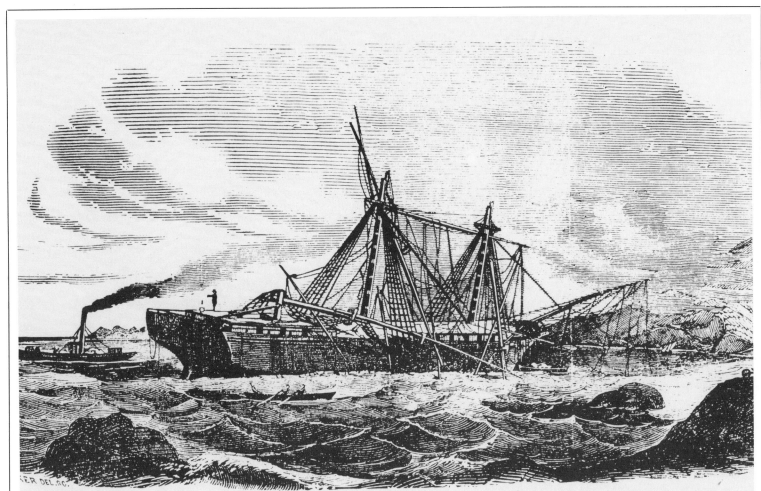

[PUBLISHED AT THE WIDE WEST OFFICE, CLAY STREET, PORTSMOUTH SQUARE.]

WRECK OF THE CLIPPER SHIP "GOLDEN FLEECE."
OFF FORT POINT, BAY OF SAN FRANCISCO.

Wreck of the clipper Golden Fleece *at Fort Point, 1854.*

Appendix 2:
Sources For Shipwreck Research

SAN FRANCISCO BAY AREA

The Bancroft Library
University of California, Berkeley
Berkeley, California 94720

The California Historical Society Library
2099 Pacific Street
San Francisco, California 94109

Federal Archives and Records Center
1000 Commodore Drive
San Bruno, California 94066

J. Porter Shaw Library
San Francisco Maritime National Historical Park
Building E, Fort Mason Center
San Francisco, California 94123

San Francisco History Room and Archives
San Francisco Public Library, Civic Center
San Francisco, California 94102

The Society of California Pioneers
456 McAllister Street
San Francisco, California 94102

ELSEWHERE IN CALIFORNIA

California Section
The California State Library
P.O. Box 2037
Sacramento, California 95809

The Henry E. Huntington Library
San Marino, California 91108

Humboldt Bay Maritime Museum
1410 Second Street
Eureka, California 95501

ELSEWHERE IN THE U.S.

The Columbia River Maritime Museum
1792 Marine Drive
Astoria, Oregon 97103

The Mariners Museum
Newport News, Virginia 23606

G.W. Blunt White Library
Mystic Seaport Museum
Mystic, Connecticut 06355

The National Archives
Washington, D.C. 20408

Naval Historical Center
Building 57
Washington Navy Yard
Washington, D.C. 20374

South Street Seaport
207 Front Street
New York, New York 10038

WHERE TO GO FOR INFORMATION ON DIVING ON SHIPWRECKS MENTIONED IN THIS BOOK:

Nearly every wreck mentioned in this book lies within the waters of the Golden Gate National Recreation Area and the Gulf of the Farallones National Marine Sanctuary. While both the National Park Service, the National Oceanic and Atmospheric Administration, and the State of California allow the public to dive on shipwrecks, divers should exercise prudent caution; most wrecks lie in extremely hazardous waters. Visibility is always limited, the currents too strong to swim against, Great White Sharks are frequent visitors, and fishing monofilament line tangles many wrecks, particularly *Frank H. Buck* and *Lyman Stewart*. This line will cut through wetsuits and flesh and a tangled diver in strong current can be seriously injured

or killed. Divers should notify the authorities if they plan to dive in a hazardous area; park rangers and police will assume you are in danger if they see people in the water off the Golden Gate.

Removal or destruction of all or part of any shipwreck within the boundary of the Golden Gate National Recreation Area is prohibited. The park's boundary extends to a quarter-mile offshore and runs along Ocean Beach, Lands End, Baker Beach, Fort Point, the Marin Headlands, and the northern Marin shore to Stinson Beach. NOAA regulations also prohibit damage or removal of portions of shipwrecks and the disturbance of the sea-bed through excavating or dredging. Both the NPS and NOAA do allow shipwreck research under permit. Permit applications are reviewed to determine the public benefit and appropriate scientific or preservation approach to historic shipwrecks.

The State of California prohibits the removal of artifacts from any shipwreck without permit. The California State Lands Commission issues permits and allows commercial salvage. Historic shipwrecks can be commercially salvaged under State law, but an archaeological approach is required. The State cannot issues permits for wrecks in the waters of the Golden Gate National Recreation Area, but can issue permits for wrecks in the marine sanctuary; these permits also require approval from NOAA before any work can proceed.

The shipwrecks at the Golden Gate, like many of California's wrecks, are submerged historical sites with archaeological value. Some are memorials and graves, others unique recreational sites offering a challenge to experienced divers. Others form artificial reefs and host marine life and communities of fish.

As this book has shown, each wreck has its own unique story. Lying on the bottom, these submerged hulks are one-of-a-kind resources that belong to the public. Divers should respect the past. Take only photographs and leave only fin kicks so that your children can see the unique story of these wrecks either on the bottom or in a museum where all can share in the past.

FOR ADDITIONAL INFORMATION, CONTACT:

Golden Gate National Recreation Area
National Park Service
Building 201, Fort Mason
San Francisco, CA 94123

Gulf of the Farallones National Marine Sanctuary
National Oceanic and Atmospheric Administration
c/o Golden Gate National Recreation Area
Building 201, Fort Mason
San Francisco, CA 94123

California State Lands Commission
1807 Thirteenth Street
Sacramento, CA 95814

State Underwater Archaeologist
California Department of Parks and Recreation
P.O. Box 94296
Sacramento, CA 94296-0001

State Historic Preservation Officer
Office of Historic Preservation
California Department of Parks and Recreation
P.O. Box 94296
Sacramento, CA 94296-0001

Bibliography

Books:

Albion, Robert G., *Square-Riggers on Schedule: The New York Sailing Packets to England, France, and the Cotton Ports.* (Princeton, New Jersey: Princeton University Press, 1938).

American Lloyd's Registry of American and Foreign Shipping. (New York: E. & G. W. Blunt, 1857-1884).

American Lloyd's Universal Standard of Shipping. (New York: Van Flee, 1857-1884).

Anonymous, *Rio Wrecking Company.* (San Francisco: Marshall Printing Company, 1901).

Bateson, Charles, *Gold Fleet for California: Forty-Niners from Australia and New Zealand.* (East Lansing: Michigan University Press, 1963).

Carrell, Toni, *Submerged Cultural Resources Inventory, Portions of Point Reyes National Seashore and Point Reyes-Farallon Islands National Marine Sanctuary: Field Research Results, Sessions 1, 1983.* (Santa Fe, New Mexico: National Park Service, 1984).

Chapelle, Howard I., *The History of American Sailing Ships.* (New York: W.W. Norton and Company, 1935).

Coman, Edwin T. Jr and Helen M. Gibbs, *Time, Tide and Timber: A Century of Pope and Talbot.* (Stanford: Stanford University Press, 1949).

Cutler, Carl C., *Queens of the Western Ocean: The Story of America's Mail and Passenger Sailing Lines.* (Annapolis, Maryland: United States Naval Institute, 1961).

Davidson, George, *Pacific Coast: Coast Pilot of California, Oregon, and Washington.* (Washington, D.C.: Government Printing Office, 1889).

Delgado, James P., *Shipwrecks of the Golden Gate.* (San Francisco: National Maritime Museum Association, 1984).

Delgado, James P., Roger Kelly, Larry Murphy, *Shipwreck Survey of a Portion of Ocean Beach, San Francisco for the United States Revenue Cutter C.W. Lawrence.* (San Francisco: National Park Service, 1984).

Delgado, James P., *To California By Sea: A Maritime History of the Gold Rush.* (Columbia: University of South Carolina Press, 1989).

Dictionary of American Fighting Ships, Vol. I. (Washington, D.C.: Government Printing Office, 1959).

Douglas, Erie, *Did She Care for Him?* (San Francisco: Philip I. Figel, 1886).

Fairburn, William Armstrong, *Merchant Sail. . . .* (Center Lovell, Maine: Fairburn Marine Educational Foundation, Inc., 1955).

Gearhart, Robert L., *Cultural Resources Magnetometer Survey and Testing: Great Highway/Ocean Beach Seawall Project, San Francisco, California.* (Austin, Texas: Espey, Huston and Associates, 1988).

Gibbs, James A., *Shipwrecks of the Pacific Coast*. (Portland, Oregon: Binfords and Mort, 1962.

Gilliam, Harold, *San Francisco Bay*. (Garden City, New York: Doubleday & Co., 1957).

Hart, James D., *A Companion to California*. (New York: Oxford University Press, 1978).

Haskins, C.W., *The Argonauts of California. . . .* (New York: Fords, Howard & Hulbert, 1890).

Hegarty, Reginald B., *Returns of Whaling Vessels Sailing from American Ports*. (New Bedford, Massachusetts: Old Dartmouth Historical Society, 1959).

Holdcamper, Forrest R., *List of American-Flag Merchant Vessels Which Received Certificates of Registry or Enrollment at the Port of New York, 1796-1869*. (Washington, D.C.: The National Archives, 1968).

Howe, Octavius T. and Frederick C. Matthews, *American Clipper Ships, 1833-1858*. (Salem, Massachusetts: Marine Research Society, 1926).

Kemble, John Haskell, *The Panama Route, 1848-1869*. (Berkeley and Los Angeles: University of California Press, 1943).

Kemble, John Haskell, *San Francisco Bay: A Pictorial Maritime History*. (Cambridge, Maryland: Cornell Maritime Press, 1957).

Langley, Henry G., *The San Francisco Directory. . . .* (San Francisco: Henry G. Langley, 1868).

Lloyds of London, *Lloyds Register of British and Foreign Shipping. . .* (London: Lloyd's, 1743-1940 passim).

Lubbock, Basil, *The Last of the Windjammers*. (Glasgow, Scotland: Brown, Son & Ferguson, Ltd., 1927).

Lubbock, Basil, *The Down Easters: American Deep-Water Sailing Ships. . . .* (Glasgow: Brown, Son & Ferguson, 1929).

Marshall, Don B., *California Shipwrecks: Footsteps in the Sea*. (Seattle: Superior Publishing Company, 1978).

Martin, Wallace E., ed. *Sail and Steam on the Northern California Coast, 1850-1900*. (San Francisco: National Maritime Museum Association, 1983).

Mason, Jack, *Point Reyes: The Solemn Land*. (Inverness, California: North Shore Books, 1970).

Mason, Jack, and Thomas J. Barfield, *Last Stage for Bolinas*. (Inverness, California: North Shore Books, 1973).

Matthews, Frederick C., *American Merchant Ships, 1850-1900*. (Salem, Massachusetts: Marine Research Society, 1931).

McNairn, Jack and Jerry MacMullen, *Ships of the Redwood Coast*. (Stanford: Stanford University Press, 1945).

Mitchell, John H., *The Commerce of the North Pacific Coast; Speech of Hon. John H. Mitchell, of Oregon, in the Senate of the United States, January 10, 1879*. (Washington, D.C.: n.p., 1879).

Munro-Fraser, J.P., *History of Marin County, California. . . .* (San Francisco: Alley, Bowen, and Company, 1880).

Murphy, Larry, ed. *Submerged Cultural Resources Survey, Portions of Point Reyes National Seashore and Point Reyes-Farallon Islands National Marine Sanctuary: Phase 1-Reconnaissance, Sessions 1 and 2, 1982*. (Santa Fe, New Mexico: National Park Service, 1984).

Randier, Jean, *Grand Voliers Francais*. (Grenoble: Edition Des Quartes Seignuers, 1974).

Rasmussen, Louis J., *San Francisco Ship Passenger Lists. Volume 1*. (Colma, California: San Francisco Historic Records, Inc., 1965).

Record of American Shipping. (New York: American Shipmasters' Association, 1886).

Ridgely-Nevitt, Cedric, *American Steamships on the Atlantic*. (Newark: University of Delaware Press, 1981).

Sawyer, L.A. and W.H. Mitchell, *The Liberty Ships*. (London and New York: Lloyd's of London Press, 1985).

Sherman, William Tecumseh, *Memoirs of William Tecumseh Sherman*. (New York: D. Appleton and Company, 1875).

Starbuck, Alexander, *History of the American Whale Fishery, From Its Earliest Inception to the year 1876*. (New York: Sentry Press, 1964).

Statutes of California, Passed at the Fifth Session of the Legislature. . . . (Sacramento: B.B. Redding, 1854).

Swann, Leonard Alexander Jr., *John Roach: Maritime Entrepreneur: The Years as Naval Contractor, 1862-1886*. (Annapolis, Maryland: United States Naval Institute, 1965).

Toogood, Anna Coxe, *A Civil History of the Golden Gate National Recreation Area*. (Denver, Colorado: National Park Service, 1980).

Toogood, Anna Coxe, *A Civil History of the Golden Gate National Recreation Area, and Point Reyes National Seashore*. (Denver, Colorado: National Park Service, 1979) 2 vols.

Throckmorton, Arthur L., *Oregon Argonauts: Merchant Adventurers on the Western Frontier*. (Portland: Oregon Historical Society, 1961).

United States Department of Commerce, *Annual List of Merchant Vessels of the United States. . . .* (Washington, D.C.: Government Printing Office, 1867-1940, passim).

United States Life-Saving Service, *Annual Report of the Operations of. . . .* (Washington, D.C.: Government Printing Office, 1878-1914 passim)

Villiers, Aland and Henri Picard, *The Bounty Ships of France*. (New York: Charles Scribner and Sons, 1972).

Works Progress Administration, *Ship Registers of New Bedford, Massachusetts. . . .* (Boston: Survey of Federal Archives, 1940).

Articles:

Anonymous, "Wreck of the Steamer *Granada*," *Hutchings' California Magazine*, V (5), November 1860.

Anonymous, "Reflections on the Causes of Shipwrecks," *The California Nautical Magazine. . . .* Vol. I, August 1862-July 1863.

Barfield, Thomas J., "SOS at Bolinas Point," *The Point Reyes Historian*, V (1), Summer 1980.

Bruce, J. Campbell, "Rescuer Extraordinary," *The Readers Digest*, March 1951.

Campbell, Esther M., "Proud Sails on Puget Sound," *Campbell Industrial Supply News*, April 1959.

Cochran, Thomas C. and Ray Ginger, "The American-Hawaiian Steamship Company, 1899-1919," *Business History Review* XXVIII (1) 1954.

Daly, R.W. and Katherine M. Daly, "Golden Gate Graveyard," *Sea Classics*, 1976.

Delgado, James P., "Underwater Archaeological Investigations of Gold Rush Era Steamships on the California Coast," *Proceedings of the First Biennial Conference on Scientific Research in California's National Parks*. (Davis: University of California, 1983).

Delgado, James P., "In the Midst of a Great Excitement: The Argosy of the Revenue Cutter *C.W. Lawrence*," *American Neptune* XLV (2) 1985.

Delgado, James P., "Shipwreck Archaeology in California: New Discoveries, New Directions," *Proceedings of the Joint Workshop New Frontiers, California State Park Rangers Association, Park Rangers Association of California, Western Interpreter's Association*, 1984.

Delgado, James P., "Documentation and Identification of the Two-Masted Schooner *Neptune*," *Historical Archaeology* CC, 1986.

Delgado, James P., "Skeleton in the Sand: Documentation of the Environmentally Exposed 1856 Ship *King Philip*," *Historical Archaeology, Special Publication No. 4*, 1986.

Delgado, James P., "Steamers to Savannah: The Origins of the New York-Savannah Steam Navigation Company," *American Neptune*.

Herz, Michael J., "Trouble on Oiled Water: Lessons from a Near-Disaster," *California WaterfrontAge*, II (2), 1986.

Kortum, Karl and Roger Olmsted, "It is a Dangerous Looking Place: Sailing Days on the Redwood Coast," *California History*, L (1), 1971.

Lyman, John, "Pacific Coast Steam Schooners, 1884-1924," *The Marine Digest*, 1943 passim.

O'Starr, Max L., "Strange Case of the Schooner William Frederick," Pacifica (California) *Tribune*, February 4, 1981.

Power, Robert H., "Maritime Artifacts in Marin: A Historic Whodunit," *California Historical Society Courier*, February 1984.

"Reflections on the Causes of Shipwrecks," *The California Nautical Magazine*, I, 1862.

Schwendinger, Robert J., "The Fearful Summer of '88: Shipwreck and Exclusion," in Benjamin F. Gilbert and K. Jack Bauer, eds. *Ports in the West.* (Manhattan, Kansas: Sunflower University Press, 1982) pp. 86-96.

Stocking, Fred, "How We Gave Tennessee Cove a Name," *Overland Monthly*, XVII (April 1891).

Storm, Fred, "Seeking the Golden Gate's Sunken Treasure," San Francisco *Examiner*, April 3, 1955.

Woolf, Alexander, "The Loss of the *Rio de Janeiro*," *Overland Monthly*, April 1901.

Manuscripts:

Aker, Raymond, "The Cermeno Expedition at Drakes Bay, 1595," Drake Navigator's Guild, Palo Alto, 1965.

Delgado, James P., "Great Leviathan of the Pacific: The Saga of the Gold Rush Steamer *Tennessee*," M.A. Thesis, East Carolina University, 1985.

Evans, Peter A., "Shipwrecks and Strandings on the Coast of Point Reyes National Seashore, 1840-140," M.A. Thesis, San Jose State College, 1969.

Frolic, United States Revenue Cutter, Logbooks, 1853, National Archives Record Group 26, Washington D.C.

LaCroix, Louis, "The Last French Cape Horners of the Nickeland Saltpeter," *Voyages of the Pacific*, Vol. 1 (1948).

Lawrence, Cornelius W., United States Revenue Cutter, Logbooks, 1848-1851, National Archives Record Group 26, Washington, D.C.

Marine Exchange (San Francisco), "Marine Disaster Ledger," unprocessed manuscript, National Maritime Museum, San Francisco.

O'Starr, Max L., "Immigrant Steamer: The Story of the *Rio de Janeiro*; The Life, Death, and the Wake of a Ship," Author, 1975.

Records of Merchant Vessel Documentation, National Archives Record Groups 36 and 41, Washington, D.C.

Records of the United States District Court, Records of the United States District Court for Northern California, Admiralty Cases, National Archives Record Group 21, Federal Archives and Records Center, San Bruno, California.

Seagamb, Inc., "Salvage and Research Design for the S.S. City of *Rio de Janeiro*," Lafayette, California, 1985.

Newspapers:

San Francisco Newspapers:

San Francisco *Bulletin*
San Francisco *Call*
San Francisco *Call-Bulletin*
San Francisco *Chronicle*
San Francisco *Daily Alta California*
San Francisco *Examiner*
San Francisco *Illustrated Daily Herald*
San Francisco *News*
San Francisco *Progress*

California Newspapers:

Coastal Post (Bolinas)
Daily Humboldt Standard (Eureka)
Humboldt Times (Eureka)
Independent Journal (San Rafael)
Los Angeles *Times*
Los Angeles *Tribune*
Marysville *Daily Appeal*
Sacramento Bee (Sacramento)
Tribune (Pacifica)
Weekly Humboldt Times (Eureka)
Weekly TImes-Telephone (Eureka)
West Coast Signal (San Francisco)

Other Newspapers and Periodicals:

The American Neptune
Daily National Intelligencer (Washington, D.C.)
Frank Leslie's Illustrated Newspaper (New York)
Sea Classics Magazine
New York *Daily Tribune*
New York *Herald*
Overland Monthly (San Francisco)
Ships and the Sea Quarterly Magazine

Glossary

Bark: A large sailing vessel, with fore-and-aft rigging on the aftermost mast, carrying square-sails on all other masts. Three-masted barks were most common, although four, and even five-masted barks were not unheard of.

Barkentine: A sailing vessel carrying square-sails on the foremast only, all other masts carried fore-and-aft rig.

Beam Ends: The beam is the width of a vessel; therefore "on her beam ends" means the vessel is at such an angle that the beam is almost at the vertical, and she is in great danger of capsizing.

Beat: To make headway against the direction of the wind, by setting a zig-zag course with the wind first off the port bow, and then the starboard.

Bight: 1) An indentation in the coastline between protruding headlands, 2) A bend in a rope taken in the process of making a knot.

Bilge: The lowest part of a vessel's interior, adjacent to the keelson.

Bowsprit: The spar protruding from the forward end of a sailing vessel.

Collier: A coal-carrying vessel.

Cutwater: The forward edge of the vessel at the waterline.

Garboard Strake: The first row of planking of a vessel's bottom.

Hawser: A large line used in towing.

Head: 1) The forward portion of a vessel, 2) A term for "headland," 3) The upper part of a triangular sail.

Howitzer: A type of cannon capable of firing a projectile directly at target, or lobbing it at an elevation up to 45 degrees.

Jibbom: The spar that extends from the bowsprit, and is used to attach the triangular headsails called jibs.

Jiggermast: The mast abaft the mizzen on a four-masted vessel.

Jibe (or Gybe): To turn a vessel away from the wind, so that she has the wind coming from the opposite end.

Kedging: Making headway by dropping an anchor some distance away from a vessel, and hauling the vessel up to it.

Keel: The "backbone" of a ship — a piece running along the bottom, upon which all the structure is supported.

Keelson: A "partner" to the keel — a major structural member running fore-and-aft in the interior of the vessel.

List: The condition of a vessel when she is in other than an upright position.

Lyle Gun: A portable gun designed to throw a lifesaving line to a vessel in distress.

Missed Stays: Failing to turn successfully from one tack to another, and coming to a standstill as the vessel's head comes into the wind.

Mizzenmast: The third mast on a vessel.

Tack: Turning a vessel into the wind, so that she sails with the wind coming from the other side; also the configuration of a vessel with the wind on either the "port tack" or the "starboard tack."

Purse-Seiner: A fishing vessel which uses a kind of net that is drawn closed around a school of fish — commonly used in sardine and tuna fisheries.

Scuppers: Drains in the bulwarks of a vessel.

Shank Painter: A rope or chain used in securing an anchor.

Stay: Rope or wire, part of the standing rigging used to brace the masts of a vessel.

Stove-In: Crushed.

Index

Author's Biographies

James P. Delgado

James P. Delgado is the Maritime Historian of the National Park Service. He supervises the NPS' maritime preservation program, which includes an ongoing inventory of historic maritime resources as well as the preparation of standards guidelines for maritime preservation work.

    Trained as both a historian and a maritime archaeologist, he has been involved with shipwreck research, survey, and excavation since 1978. He has published more than fifty articles and four books. He has also nominated more than seventy-five historic sites, buildings, and structures (mostly ships and shipwrecks) to the National Register of Historic Places.

Stephen A. Haller

Stephen A. Haller is presently the Curator of Historic Documents for the San Francisco Maritime National Historical Park and the Golden Gate National Recreation Area. He studied nineteenth century American history at the University of Rochester, and has specialized in the study of shipwrecks and the naval and military history of World War II. He lives with his family in El Cerrito, California, where he enjoys hiking, exploring, and bird watching in his spare time.

The photographs used in this book are supplied courtesy of the following individuals and organizations:

Bancroft Library, U.C. Berkeley: 12, 59

Columbia River Maritime Museum, Astoria, Oregon: 16

Gleason's Pictorial Drawing Room Companion: 115

Golden Gate National Recreation Area: 54

National Archives, Record Group 26, U.S. Coast Guard: XIX, XXI

National Park Service, James Delgado, Photographer: 132, 136, 139, 147

National Park Service, Edward de St. Maurice, Photographer: 135

Peabody Museum of Salem: 29

San Francisciana, Marilyn Blaisdell: 73

San Francisco Maritime National Historical Park: V, VI, IX, X, XV, XVI, 19, 26, 31, 34, 36, 38, 45, 47, 49, 50, 52, 61, 62 65, 67, 68, 74, 75, 77, 78, 81, 83, 85, 90, 94, 100, 105, 116, 119, 122, 124, 127, 129, 130

San Francisco Public Library: 6, 41, 42, 44, 97

Mary Ann Stets, Mystic Seaport, Mystic, CT.: 143